BREATHING AND

WALKING AROUND

MERCER
UNIVERSITY PRESS

Endowed by
TOM WATSON BROWN
and
THE WATSON-BROWN FOUNDATION, INC.

BREATHING AND

WALKING AROUND

Meditations on a Life

Kathy A. Bradley

MERCER UNIVERSITY PRESS
MACON, GEORGIA

MUP/P442
P442e

© 2012 Mercer University Press
1400 Coleman Avenue
Macon, Georgia 31207
All rights reserved

First Edition

2nd Printing, May 2012

Books published by Mercer University Press are printed on acid-free paper that
meets the requirements of American National Standard for Information
Sciences—Permanence of Paper for Printed Library Materials.

Mercer University Press is a member of Green Press Initiative
(greenpressinitiative.org), a nonprofit organization working to help publishers
and printers increase their use of recycled paper and decrease their use of fiber
derived from endangered forests. This book is printed on recycled paper.
ISBN 13:   978-0-88146-270-8
ISBN 10:   0-88146-270-5
e-book 13: 978-088146-363-7
ISBN 10:   0-88146-363-9
Cataloging-in-Publication Data is available from the Library of Congress

ACKNOWLEDGMENTS

I had a friend whose habit was to say thank you over and over for the same kindness. Eventually I broke him of the habit by repeatedly responding with, "Once is sufficient." It does seem to me that one thank you, genuinely extended, should be enough and, if repeated, could possibly be interpreted as not having been sincere in the first place.

Risking, then, the possibility that any one or more of the following people could think that my previously extended thanks were anything less than sincere, I feel compelled to offer public acknowledgment of the contributions each of them as made to this book and to the journey that birthed it.

I hit the lottery when it came to parents. Johnny and Frances Anderson Bradley taught me by example everything I needed to know about how to live a meaningful life and their fingerprints are scattered over every one of these pages.

My nephew and niece, Adam and Kate, could do little about my invasion of their privacy as children. I wrote about them with outrageous pride and without a second thought. As adults, they have, I think, forgiven and continue to indulge me. Watching them grow taught me more than I could have ever imagined. (And, yes, Kate, without your Skype-yell this book would not exist. I owe you.)

I cannot imagine how different my life would be had Katherine not decided she wanted to be my friend. Thank you, KP, for that single act of courage and all the acts since.

Margaret Duckworth Sewell's e-mail syndicate of my newspaper columns was my first indication that people who didn't even know me found my words worth reading. The Saint Queen Mum is a treasure. Lauren King Bolin and Lea-King Badyna are cheerleaders of the best kind—they know when to pull and when to stop pulling and start pushing.

I seriously doubt that anyone has ever had so great a cloud of witnesses accompany her along a journey of this sort as have I. Along with those otherwise mentioned, these folks are the best friends a girl could ever have: The Buckeyes (Margaret, Susan, Gena, Mary Catherine, and Anne); Penny and Jim; Jason; Debra and Mike; Robin; Gaye; Julie and Ted; Melissa; Sandra Kate; Daphne (she of the parallel path); cousin Diane; Becky; Lynn; Helen Anne; Phyllis and David; Mandy V.; and Kay.

The clan into which I was born is a large and noisy one and I owe them more than the genes for green eyes and the space between my two front teeth. It was within the safety of their bosom that I learned to tell stories. Thank you to my brother Keith, Grannie, Pa, Grandmama, Granddaddy, and all the aunts and uncles and cousins. To the Bradley Girls (Aunt June, Katherine, Diane, Debbie and Donna), here's to tradition and sparkling grape juice.

Jackson is the first of his generation on our branch of the family tree. He reminds me why we tell the stories. Thank you, Jenn and Adam, for making me a great-aunt.

The past and current editors of the Statesboro Herald— Larry Anderson, Amelia Morrison Hipps, the late Nancy Welch, and Jim Healey—provided me with a forum and took me back after I left. Rheneta Washington Ward deserves thanks for her attentive proofreading and, more importantly, for the constant affirmation.

My past and current bosses, R.J. Martin, III and Richard A. Mallard, District Attorneys of the Ogeechee Judicial Circuit, both exhibited great tolerance of my extra-curricular activity and that tolerance is a big part of how this all happened.

Marc Jolley and the staff of Mercer University Press made the publication part far easier than I'd been led to believe it would be. They are very good at what they do.

One final note: Some of my family and many friends are identified by name in this book; some are not. There are reasons for each. Those in both groups understand why.

Kathy A. Bradley
March 2012

BREATHING AND

WALKING AROUND

INTRODUCTION

> Take some thread of yourself—say it is your ability to love—put your finger on it and trace it back in time. Not far, and your finger finds a lump, a bump, a tangle, a ganglion. Here the thread loops back on itself, encircles and chokes itself, convolutes till you know: it is a knot.
>
> Now you can begin to pull, and you learn ... how the limpsy string becomes a nubbin, a recalcitrant, tiny, in-laced rock, and with each impatient tug you convert energy into a minute hardness. You cannot make a knot unloose itself with this external force; no, you can make it smaller, but you cannot make it disappear. ...
>
> Oh, mankind, you must learn to tat if you would live content. The thread of yourself must form a knobby loop that takes in a larger, growing shape. ...
>
> Let me know that into the knot of self comes the thread called time, and that what I am ... came from what I was, goes to what I yet may be.
>
> —*Ahab's Wife*, Sena Jeter Naslund

Observation is the first step. And with the observation, one can begin to articulate the truth.

I did not always know this.

I was smart and educated. I read good books and listened to good music. I engaged in conversation of all sorts. I laughed a lot and, on occasion, indulged myself in what could only be called, in a woman of my age, pure silliness.

I would have told anyone who asked that I was attentive and wakeful, easily awed and frequently amazed. I noticed and noted trees as they bloomed and children as they grew. I was not, as the frequently needlepointed cliché offered, so busy with making a living that I forgot to make a life.

And, yet, I lived as though my contact lenses needed cleaning and I was afraid to take them out long enough to do the job.

In elementary school I was the first one in the class to finish the standardized tests. My teacher would walk quietly to my desk, lean forward, and whisper, "Don't you want to look back over your answers?"

"No, ma'am," I would whisper back with a polite smile.

I was sure, very sure, that what I knew was all I knew and all I knew was all there was to know. Looking back over the flimsy test booklet and stiff answer sheet would not change that.

If my childhood could be reduced to one image, it is this one.

From the time I learned to create letters and turn letters into words, I wrote. Stories about talking animals became poems about teenage angst became essays and journal entries that college professors assigned with some hope, I assume, of discovering a person inside the caricature I so often felt I was.

I stopped writing when I started law school. The documents I produced in the pursuit of a law degree—the briefs, the memos, the pleadings—rolled out of the electric typewriter I'd received as a college graduation gift from my parents in a rising tide of anxiety and deadlines. I cut and pasted, literally, the words and ideas of far better minds than mine and used Strunk and White to sand down the edges so that the ebbing tide was gentle and lulling. I received awards for what was technically good, but passionless.

It was fifteen years later that I told my friend Phyllis a story about an odd piece of legislation that had just come out of the Georgia General Assembly. A week or so later, at a lunch meeting in our small town, she asked me to repeat the story to her friend Larry.

Larry was, at the time, the editor of the newspaper and, upon hearing the story, asked if I'd be willing to write it down so he could publish it. I did. He did.

A few weeks later I wrote another piece. A month or so later, another one.

2

After the third, Larry called and asked what it would take to get me to do it on a regular basis. I almost said, "Not much." Instead, I said, "Let me think about it."

For the next seven years, more or less, I delivered to Larry and then his successors a biweekly column. It wasn't Erma Bombeck and it wasn't Ellen Goodman. It was simply me—me telling stories about my niece and nephew who were growing up next door, me telling stories about living on the family farm, me telling stories about living as an adult in the same community in which I'd grown up.

The writing was effortless. There were no citations to authority. There were no words like "heretofore" and "notwithstanding." There were only words that shimmered like pearls strung together on a silver chain.

People seemed to like the words. Sometimes, at the grocery store or the baseball field, I would be recognized from the postage stamp-sized photo that accompanied the column and someone would stop me to share his own story or to tell me that she liked mine. I made them, people whose voices were thick with my same drawl, feel comfortable and I liked that.

In December 2003, when I'd been writing my predictable column for seven years, my best friend stood on my front porch and, in a tone both smooth and trembling, asked me to marry him. I said yes.

I was forty when we met, about the same time I started writing the column, and it took those seven years before either of us was willing to admit to anyone, including ourselves, that we were more than friends. When we finally did, the proposal arriving shortly on the heels of his return from a three-month stay abroad during which we'd both tried unsuccessfully to display a measured nonchalance about our separation, the world of our families and friends erupted into a shower of joy and relief.

Two weeks after our engagement announcement had appeared in the newspaper, my best friend stretched out on the couch in my living room and told me, in the same tone he used on the porch three months prior, that he couldn't marry me.

The next morning I canceled the tuxedo rentals, the photographer, the caterer, and the church reservation. I couldn't cancel the invitations; they'd already been printed. I picked them up the next day and drove them around in the back seat of my car for a month trying to figure out what to do with them. The dress for which I'd already paid would be delivered in about three weeks; one of my friends would pick it up and keep it in her closet for six months.

There were other things I had to do. One of them was to call the newspaper and tell the editor that I would not be writing the column anymore.

It's interesting being a small-town pseudo-celebrity. People think they know you when they don't. They take liberties that your closest friends would not take. They want to know why you're not writing anymore. They tell you how much they miss you. And, when word gets out that there will be no wedding announcement following up on that engagement announcement, they think it's perfectly all right to stop you in the Wendy's parking lot and ask you why you didn't get married.

For the next year and a half I wrote nothing except embarrassingly painful journal entries and overly sincere thank-you notes to the diligent friends who watched over me as I tried to regain my footing.

I was forty-seven when this happened. At twenty-two or twenty-five or even thirty, I suspect that I would have recovered more quickly. The heart, like the face, loses elasticity with age.

In the fall of the second year while visiting with one of those diligent friends, she asked why I wasn't writing and, in response to my non-answer, said something about the sadness of a gift going unused. Upon hearing the words that I remember now only in a general sense, I felt something turn. Metaphorically speaking, it could have been a corner in an unfamiliar city or the key to a long-locked door. Whatever it was, it forced me, upon my return home, to call my contact at the newspaper and ask if they would take me back.

Fortunately for me, they said yes.

So I began again, the column both exactly the same as before and not at all as it was before. The frequency and word length remained about the same. There were still stories about children and dogs and the cycling seasons, but there was a difference.

I assumed that I would, as before, simply offer a tale, a yarn, an anecdote to an audience I hoped was still willing to listen to it. And from that simple exchange I would receive satisfaction. That is not, however, what happened. The act of writing week after week, month after month, year after year became, I discovered, an attempt to figure out how so many of those carefully colored-in ovals on the answer sheet had been wrong.

This is the record of that attempt.

I resumed writing just in time for Christmas and it seemed, of course, less coincidence than purposeful serendipity. I am Christian by heritage and choice and beginning again in step with the church calendar seemed somehow not just appropriate, but essential to the sense I was hoping to make.

The words here are, then, arranged chronologically and the different themes are simply separate curves that run the length of the time line, undulating and occasionally crossing each other. Sometimes the curves shape themselves into clearly discernible images; sometimes they are just curves, a trail moving unpredictably into territory that is both wild and familiar.

Writing is the attempt of one person to bear witness. When it is done honestly and well, the attempt, whatever the form, will unearth not answers, but questions. The questions came before us and will remain long after we are gone.

DECEMBER 18, 2005

The season is upon us. Advent. Preparation.

It is time to cut the tree, dust off the ornaments, and make the lists. Time to check the calendar and sign the cards and wrap the gifts. Time to stand in line and stop in traffic. Time to get it all done in time.

Christians have been observing Advent since sometime around the fourth century. My own observance is a relatively new one. I am still burning the original purple and rose candles that came with the wreath that now sits in the middle of my kitchen table.

The sun will soon disappear behind the pine trees at the edge of the farm. The silvery gray of late autumn will settle over Sandhill like a blanket and nighttime will begin its predictable creep over the landscape, into my thoughts.

I am wondering why I am doing this. What difference it can possibly make.

I pull out a chair and, spurred by what is quite possibly nothing more than guilt, promise myself that this year I will be diligent. I will not get too busy to light each candle in its turn. I will—on the first and second and third and fourth Sundays of Advent—calm myself, still myself, give myself the time to reflect.

Holding the match over the matchbox, I look at the unlit candles. The wicks are black and brittle. Lines of dripping wax have marred their colors with uneven streaks. One tilts just a bit to the side despite my best efforts to straighten it. They remind me that—despite the frivolity and gaiety, the bells and carols, the goodwill and neighborliness in which we cloak ourselves this time of year—it was not into a world of light that the Messiah came, but a world of darkness.

Every day brought the drudgery of political oppression, religious persecution, and economic despair. The past was a sad indictment of the Jews' failure as a people. The future promised nothing but more of the same.

For four thousand years they had been waiting. In darkness. The words they rehearsed in their children's ears had become dull in the repetition. The memorials of stone they had built had been lost in the years of wind and rain and neglect. Did anyone still believe? Could anyone still believe?

And at that moment, into the silence came the voice of an angel. A divine herald, a prophetic courier with words of promise and hope, a message to the world that what is now is not what will always be. A message for all the world.

But the only one who heard it, the single soul with whom Gabriel shared the news, was one simple girl. No one else. Not the High Priest or the commander of the occupying army. Not the ruling governor or a learned scribe. Just a simple girl with a wild imagination.

Wild enough to stay there and listen to the messenger angel call her things like "highly favored" and "blessed." Wild enough to listen to him tell her she was going to be the mother of the long-awaited, nearly-forgotten Messiah. Wild enough to believe.

Twenty-first-century Americans aren't all that different from first-century Palestinians, I think. I am no different. I, we struggle with our past failures, wrestle with current crises, worry about a future we can't predict. What will it take for us—for me—to see through the darkness?

Only one thing. The same thing it took for Mary. Call it a wild imagination or call it faith. Either way, it requires eyes that see the invisible. Ears that hear something in the silence. Hands that extend in the direction of the irrational, the impossible, the unthinkable.

I pause, breathe deeply, strike the match. I light the first candle. The flame leaps up, flickers, steadies itself. Across the room the small light reappears, a reflection in the window. The solitary candle becomes two and in the window beside it three and then four.

The candle of hope. Hope that the darkness will not always envelop the earth. Hope that the promise will be fulfilled. Hope that each heart that still listens will echo the whispered assent of the simple girl: Be it done unto me according to thy word.

Amen.

JANUARY 1, 2006

Hard to believe it is January already. It startles me every year—like a calico cat, languid and unobtrusive, moving along the edges of the room, clearly visible but not really noticeable, suddenly pouncing into my lap with a look that says, "I know you don't like me. That is why, out of all the people in this room, I chose you."

The fields on either side of Sandhill are empty. The cornstalks and peanut vines that occupied long and even rows for so much of the year have disappeared, their fruit long harvested, their skeletal remains burned off and turned under by loud and heavy machines.

The year winds down and the land does nothing. It produces no crop. It provides no cover for rabbits and mice and snakes. It simply is.

I stare out the window at the emptiness. In the sudden halt to activity in the days after Christmas, I keep thinking that there must be something that needs doing. I am looking for something that intrigues me, tells me a story, drives away the chill, but I feel myself becoming frustrated with the silence of a farm asleep.

It is hard sometimes to find beauty in the India-ink silhouettes of empty trees, the long black shadows of sagging fence posts, the black-and-white sky.

I remember a song from a Judy Collins CD I got one Christmas. "I'll learn to love the fallow way," she sings in that trembling soprano. "When winter draws the valley down and stills the rivers in their storm and freezes all the little brooks."

Is it possible that I could do that? Learn to love the fallow way?

"Fallow" is a word that doesn't get used much these days. It is a word for farmers and poets, mostly. An adjective, its primary definition is "left untilled or unsown after plowing." It also means "dormant" or "inactive." Easy to see why our drive-thru, one-hour, speed-obsessed, convenience-driven society wouldn't think much of such a word.

What a shame. For it is not only land that needs to be left untilled on occasion. Lying fallow can also be good, I think, for the human heart.

What would it take, I wonder, to allow myself to lie fallow for a while?

I would, like the land, have to yield myself to the fire that burns away the stubble, the broken stalks and dried-up vines that, having borne their fruit, do nothing but clutter the surface.

I would, like the land, have to allow myself to be turned and plowed up, the rocks and roots brought to the surface and carted away.

I would, like the land, have to be quiet and still, having nothing to do but wait.

The burning, the turning, is not so difficult when one reaches a certain age. But the waiting—that never gets any easier. Can I do that?

The fields on either side of Sandhill will not be empty for long. Already Daddy is making plans, repairing machinery, watching the sky. Soon the tractors will be grinding their way across the acres, etching deep furrows into the soil, pulling the planters that will drop the seeds.

The song goes on: "As sure as time, as sure as snow, as sure as moonlight, wind and stars, the fallow time will fall away. The sun will bring an April day and I will yield to summer's way."

I open the curtain a little wider. There is a promise hovering in the cold gray air, a promise that, for the one who is willing to surrender, the fallow time is hard, but never long.

JANUARY 8, 2006

The Saturday morning that I finally tackled the cleaning out of the attic, I found myself surrounded by a rug rolled into a long cigar, a doll cradle, Christmas tree stands of various sizes, a cooler, and probably twenty-five cardboard boxes, some of them mislabeled. Wreaths hung from the rafters by ten-penny nails and insulation billowed up from the unfloored part of the attic like cotton candy.

I stood in the dim light of one naked overhead bulb and wondered how I would decide which of the thousands of pieces of my history would stay and which would go. I was torn between wanting to toss everything blindly and wanting to go through every box, every file to make sure I wasn't getting rid of something important.

The boxes stacked on top of each other contained everything from old canceled checks to a wall calendar from 1975. In one of them was my Girl Scout badge sash, in another old school notebooks. There were doll clothes and 8-track tapes and scrapbooks with pages nibbled along the edges by mice.

Two large trash bags and six or seven trips up and down the attic stairs later, I had reached a compromise with myself. There had been some tossing, some tears, and a lot of restacking. The attic was, as a result, neater but not a whole lot emptier.

I thought about that the other day when Aden's mom called to tell me about Christmas. At four, she shared, he finally "got it." And what she meant by that was that the excitement this year was his own, not just a reflection of his family's. He spent all day Christmas Eve going back and forth to the computer with his dad, charting Santa's progress around the world. "He's in Peru!" he cried out running through the living room and then, an hour later, "He's in Mexico!"

On Christmas morning he went outside and found a single jingle bell in the yard. He picked it up, dark brown eyes shining, and said in near-disbelief, "It still smells like reindeer."

Ah, I couldn't help smiling when she told me that. I could just see him holding the shiny jingle bell in his little boy hand and staring at it with that special brand of awe that exists exclusively in childhood and fades so slowly that one realizes it is gone only too late to halt the progress.

"It still smells like reindeer." And I knew, then, why I'd never be able to throw away the key chain, the note scribbled on the paper plate, the name tag, the smooth gray stone, the newspaper clippings. Each one, held in my hand and up to the light, conjures up a memory. Each one still smells like reindeer.

Jingle bell awe exists only in childhood, but there is another kind that is available to even the most grown-up of grown-ups. It is the astonishing realization that even as our vision narrows to focus on those things like meetings and mortgages, to concentrate more and more on that which we can manage, govern, or manipulate, our other senses, like those of the blind, can become more sensitive. It is the amazing revelation that we can still hear jingle bells and smell reindeer as long as we remember. And we will remember as long as there are tokens and talismans, relics and artifacts. As long as our attics and desk drawers and hall closets hold the keepsakes of our hearts.

I suspect that the jingle bell will be around for a long time. Will probably make its way into a box, into an attic at some point. And then one day, when someone is seeking righteous cleanliness, it will reappear, dull and rusted, and, rolling it around in his hand, Aden will be reminded of the Christmas he was four years old, the Christmas he tracked Santa Claus across South America and learned what it meant to believe.

JANUARY 15, 2006

One of the first things Mama did after following through on her long-promised, long-awaited retirement was to commission the construction of a fence around her yard. She said she was hoping that the fence might discourage Lily and Tamar from chasing cars. She was also hoping, I think, to slow the encroachment of corn and peanut fields. Like the wind and water that gradually eat away at the beach, leaving only a narrow strip of sand and sea oats, the plow and harrow tend to imperceptibly inch their way into grass and flower beds.

The commission for this important restoration effort was given to what can only be described as (and I do this with great love) a motley crew.

The foreman was Daddy, whose construction motto is "That's good enough." Assisting him were Keith, who unlike many men practices a clean-up-as-you-go building creed, and Adam, who contributed the brute strength of a six-foot-four-inch twenty-three-year-old and the constant irritation of his brutal sense of humor by repeatedly flavoring the process with comments like, "You know, Gu, I'm enjoying this so much I'm thinking I might just quit college and start me a fence-building business." Father, son, and grandson, three generations that could not by the stretch of the wildest imagination be considered a trinity anywhere near holy.

The yard is not large and the fence as designed by Mama is not complicated. These elements, however, did not prevent the project from becoming a month-long venture. At least three times it appeared to my untrained eye to have been completed and at least three times I would come by the house to find a section being taken down and rebuilt, Mama's dressmaker's eye having detected some aesthetic flaw that simply would not do.

Let it be said that during the entire process my position remained that of Switzerland—interested, but neutral. Not that my affiliation for one side or the other was not courted. No, on more than one occasion one or the other of my parents would engage in a little eye-rolling or whispered exasperation, but after watching the two of them navigate life's large and small aggravations for over fifty years without significant interference on my part, I am smart enough to smile and quickly change the subject. Like Br'er Rabbit, I laid low.

Eventually the fence was completed to Mama's satisfaction and Daddy's relief, and all the people said, "Amen."

The twenty-first century does not afford families the opportunity to work together very often. Most people don't live near enough to their parents or siblings to participate in each other's home improvement projects and, even if they did, they don't know each other well enough to be able to work through the inevitable irritations that arise whenever hammers and nails are involved. Most people have never built a fence; they just live inside one.

Just the other morning as I drove by the completed project on my way to work, I noticed the straight lines, the sharp corners, the sturdy posts, the way the early morning sunlight cast awkward angled shadows on the dry winter grass. A good strong fence.

I was reminded of the line from Robert Frost's "Mending Wall": "Good fences make good neighbors." I laughed. That might be true where Mr. Frost lived, but here in the country where my family has congregated the truer word is that good fences are made by good neighbors. And the best neighbors are the ones who share your name.

JANUARY 29, 2006

Fog, Carl Sandburg said, comes in on little cat feet. That may be true in Chicago, land of tall towers, skyscrapers built to bend with the wind, but at Sandhill fog doesn't creep. It is more like a wooly blanket being shaken from its folds by a quick pop of the wrists and draping itself over the body of a sleeping child. Swift and total.

Fog in the country, a place of few artificial lights and wide swathes of open field, can be disconcerting. Without the interior compass of someone who has long lived in the isolation, it could be maddening, even if only temporarily, and more than a little frightening.

The other morning I woke to such a fog—thick and heavy, like a bolt of gray-blue satin flung across the fields, undulating in inconsistent waves. Tiny dots of moisture clung to the window screens like glass beads. The mist hovered in the air, like rain in suspended animation.

I sat in my reading chair and stared at the unconventional loveliness. The day was beginning not with clarity and sharp focus but with uneven edges and smudged lines, illegible instructions, and, unlike the self that at one time would have been frustrated if not downright bewildered by such imprecision and uncertainty, the self of now simply took a deep breath, allowed her shoulders to relax, and felt the soft cushions of the chair accept the weight of my body and my thoughts.

I will be fifty on my next birthday. Asking me to read the eye chart projected onto the wall in the exam room, Whit laughingly tells me I have the eyes of a forty-year-old. No bifocals yet. The only symptom of advancing eye age is the necessity of an extra blink or two when moving from focus on the near to the distant. Or the distant to the near. And I wonder, is that a handicap or an evolutionary advantage?

I have never been impulsive, but at twenty or even thirty I always felt the pressure to prompt and decisive action on whatever question was placed to me. Where would I attend college? What would be my major? Should I take that job? Which of the applicants should I hire?

But slowly I began to understand the value of the extra blink. I began to understand the advantage of the deep breath before speaking, the wisdom of knowing that days and minutes will pass without any effort on my part and the answers to most of life's big questions come unbidden and in their own time. I learned to live in fog.

I get up from the chair and dress for church. Between the noise of the shower and the hair dryer I hear bits and pieces of the radio news broadcast. I stop long enough to listen to the entire piece on Bill Hancock, a college administrator who wrote *Riding With The Blue Moth*, a memoir of a cross-country bike trip he took in the aftermath of his thirty-something son's death in a plane crash. I smile. A fellow traveler, someone else who has learned to value the extra blink, someone else who has learned to live in fog.

The sky has lightened some as I leave the house. More silver than gray, like polished pewter, simultaneously shiny and dull. I still cannot see the sycamore tree in Mama and Daddy's backyard and I have to feel my way slowly down the back steps to avoid stumbling in the dimness, but slowly does not mean fearfully. I will reach the bottom eventually. And at the bottom is solid ground.

FEBRUARY 12, 2006

The Baltimore airport has an indoor playground. At least it did until major renovations started last summer and construction barriers and "do not cross" police tape replaced the airplane and train that had been the salvation of many an adult with a delayed flight.

I learned this last September when I flew north to celebrate Aden's third birthday. My plane arrived a couple of hours before his Aunt Lea's so the plan was for Aden, his mom, and me to hang out at the playground until the flight from Jacksonville arrived. Rounding the corner of one of the endless corridors that make modern airports look like mazes and passengers feel like neurotic mice, we found not brightly colored walls and a room full of toddlers, but huge sheets of plastic and one of those "pardon our mess as we progress" signs.

And so, in the only way that a three-year-old knows how to express the simultaneously felt emotions of immense grief and total frustration, the towheaded angel began to cry.

And I couldn't blame him. Counting the drive time to Savannah and the layover in Atlanta I'd been sitting for about eight hours. I'd had nothing to eat all day except expensive airport food and my ears hadn't quite recovered from the descent into BWI that always leaves my head feeling as though my brain has swollen beyond the size of my skull. I wanted to cry, too.

But I didn't. I just knelt down so that I was level with those huge chocolate eyes floating in water and said, "You know what we need to do, A? We need to complain. We need to let these airport people know how unhappy we are that they closed our playground."

Aden blinked and a couple of huge tears rolled down his cheeks. He stopped crying and stared at me, a little unsure what I was talking about.

"Yep, I think that's what we need to do. Make a formal complaint." I pulled out my Day-Timer and found a blank sheet and a pen. "Sit down right here, A, and help me write this letter."

A bit confused, but more curious, he sat down and stared at my hand moving across the page in big block letters. "Dear Airport Man: My name is Aden Bolin and I am three years old. I am very disappointed that you closed my playground. Please open it again soon." I handed him the pen to sign the letter and he scribbled a reasonable facsimile of a signature at the bottom.

By this time all evidence of toddler meltdown had evaporated, replaced by a look (to which I am not unaccustomed) of quizzical amusement.

"So now we need to go find Somebody In Charge," I announced, handing the letter to the cherub and tossing him onto my hip. We waved goodbye to Mom and took off through the airport looking for Somebody In Charge. Up one escalator, down the long and wide row of ticket counters Aden and I scoured the faces of people in uniform for the one to whom we could entrust delivery of our letter.

There was no line at one of the stations at the Southwest counter. We walked up to a pleasant-looking young man and handed him the letter. "You look like Somebody In Charge," I said.

"Well, actually, um, I'm...."

"Yes," I said pointedly and tilted my head toward Aden. "You look like Somebody In Charge and we'd like to give you this letter to deliver to the Airport Man. Our playground is closed and we're very sad about that and we want the Airport Man to open it up again."

"Uh, well, of course. I happen to know the man who is in charge of the whole airport and I'll be very glad to see he gets this letter."

We thanked the gentleman and we, one slightly deranged woman and one delighted and tear-free child, went skipping back to baggage claim.

I thought about that the other day when I became frustrated with one of those silly things that tend to make grown men and women behave like three-year-olds. Thought about how important it is to acknowledge what we feel, how important it is to speak our pain, and how very very important it is to be able to turn it all over to Somebody In Charge.

FEBRUARY 26, 2006

When I was a little girl I heard Daddy tell a story, a parable really, about the boy who was plowing a field and kept ending up with crooked rows. In frustration he went to his father and asked, "What am I doing wrong?"

"Are you giving yourself something to watch all the way down the row?"

"Yes, sir, just like you told me."

"What are you watching?"

"I'm watching that black and white cow in the next field."

"Son," the exasperated but very wise father told him, "watching a moving target ain't never gonna get you a straight row."

A long time ago I had a secretary who had been an art major in college. One day we were making a banner for some completely non-work-related purpose and I watched her cut a perfectly straight line from one side of the banner to the other. I was amazed.

"How in the world did you do that?" I asked her.

"How did I do what?"

"Cut that straight line without marking it."

"Easy," she said. "You don't look at your hand or the scissors. You keep your eye on where you want to end up."

There is something about straightness that appeals to our Western sensibility. It connotes order and civility. We call a forthright person a straight shooter. When we want a question answered in the briefest, clearest terms possible we say we want to hear it straight up. We learn in Sunday School that "strait is the gate, and narrow is the way." Through what gate and to what way it leads we are not always sure, but the weight and authority of straightness fused with narrowness leaves us with the conviction that it must be something worth pursuing.

Kathy A. Bradley

Velma Kemp was my high school geometry teacher. She devoted her life to teaching children how to compute circumference and radius and the area of a circle. She taught us the difference between acute and obtuse angles, the distinction between perpendicular and parallel lines.

The very first concept to which Miss Kemp introduced us was the idea that the shortest distance between two points is a straight line. It was a most appealing idea to us competitive, goal-oriented, headed-for-college-and-then-on-to-change-the-world teenagers. To get from here to there in the most efficient manner we need only look straight ahead and keep our eyes on a stationery target, not a grazing cow, not our hands nor the scissors we held in them.

But life isn't straight. It has a way of curving in sharp and unexpected ways. It wanders aimlessly for a moment and, suddenly, takes off like a spooked horse. It moves you gently along for years, past all the reassuring landmarks listed on MapQuest, and then abruptly leaves you at the end of the asphalt. Or you look up one day at scenery that is very familiar and realize you've been traveling in circles.

So much for order and civility. The whole thing is apt to make a person wonder if there is any reason to be straight, go straight, tell it straight, or straighten up and fly right.

Unless, of course, one remembers the second concept Miss Kemp so generously offered up to us Philistines: A straight line is the only kind of line there is. An arc, a circle, a curve in the road is simply an infinite number of straight lines.

Life doesn't always look straight or feel straight. But it can be when each day, each moment, is its own straight line. Lines that are drawn by a hand directed by an eye fixed on something that doesn't move.

MARCH 12, 2006

It is a late afternoon in March. The sky is changing color. From clear blue to pale lavender and smoky amethyst. The highway, a satin ribbon of gray asphalt, unrolls beneath the tires of cars and trucks taking people home. Work is over. Supper waits. It is as though the landscape itself sighs with the fatigue of another day done.

Around a curve the light changes, the color fades. Choking gray smoke races across the horizon like a startled deer. Somewhere nearby somebody is burning off a field.

It is that time of year. Time to get the fields ready. Time to rid them of the debris of last year's crop. Time to destroy all that is left of the past failure or success and start over. Time to start the cycle all over again—plant, water, harvest, burn.

Despite the speed with which the flames consume the dry stalks and leaves, burning off fields is slow, meticulous work. The process never changes. The strike of a match. The touch of flame to brittle vine. The contagion that spreads the heat down what used to be perfectly parallel, neatly lined rows. The cautious watching, the slow amble along the edges of the field to make sure that the fire remains contained.

It is never the height of a field fire that must be tended. The flames stay low, a shimmering halo, a flickering crown atop a broad black face. The breadth, though, that is what must be watched with vigilance. The dirt road that should halt its progress, the pond that is its boundary, the fire break whose very reason for existence is to hem in the blaze is never unfailingly reliable. Anything could happen.

I can stand on my porch and watch the process. Like an army of tiny orange-clad soldiers the fire advances on the dead vegetation. It disintegrates into flat blackness and the bitter, stinging smell of sulphur that will linger long into the night. The smoke that rises in the wake of the destruction makes no sound.

I am mesmerized. Pyromania seems, for the moment, not such a bad thing.

I remember once when I was still living at home that Daddy came in after having burned off a field and, in the manner of farmers, forgot to leave his boots by the door. Across the carpet, Mama's carpet, he walked, obliviously leaving a trail of black shoe-shaped prints behind him. I have done that myself, I think— walked through destruction and left its imprint on something that had been clean.

The fire goes out. It has behaved well this time and left behind nothing but acres and acres of ashes.

A few days ago I stood in church and had ashes placed on my forehead. Messy, sooty, smutty ashes.

"Remember, Kathy," the minister said as he placed his thumb on my forehead and streaked it black with the sign of the cross, "it is from dust that thou hast come and it is to dust that thou wilt return."

It is a somber thought, the idea that I will become nothing more than ashes. That this body that has felt the warmth of sunshine and the tickle of a feather, that has been rocked by the ocean and the breeze off a lake will one day disintegrate, will be burned off like just another field.

I drive home in silence. Pulling into the driveway at Sandhill where the stars are shining like new diamonds and the grass that is trying to turn green is already damp with dew, I am aware without articulation that I am a part of the cycle. Plant, water, harvest, burn.

MARCH 26, 2006

It was dark when I got home the other night. Long day. The kind of day that leaves you distracted, glad that there is a part of your mind that can drive without a lot of conscious effort. My thoughts were far away.

I pulled up to the mailbox, the one whose door rusted off years ago. Driving a different car, I couldn't find the button/knob/lever that would turn on the inside lights. I growled at nobody in particular and, hoping I wouldn't drop a bill or a sale paper or a catalog and have to get out of the car to retrieve it, reached through the window into the dark mouth of the mailbox.

Pause that scene for a moment.

It's been about four springs since the bird's nest appeared in the mailbox. At first I thought it was just a mass of dried grass thrust into the metal cave by the March winds that had come to dry out the fields after the winter rains, but it got bigger and took on a shape and then, one day, as I was pulling up to get the mail, a bird came dashing out and landed on the power line just overhead.

From that point, I was very careful about checking my mail. I didn't try to get a look at the eggs, didn't touch the nest. The mama bird and I developed an understanding: she would ignore the mail and allow me access to it as long as I ignored her and her babies.

Birds aren't supposed to return to nests year after year. At least that's what I've been told. This bird has. Or, if it isn't the same bird, she has gotten into real estate management and sub-let to a series of other young mothers.

Release pause.

Just as my hand touched the stack of mail a mad flutter of wings erupted and the bird flew directly into my face. Frightened and crazed, she beat her wings against my cheek. Frightened and crazed, I tried to move away from her within the confined space of the front seat of the car.

She followed me in and, as I managed to get the door open so that a light would come on, she began flying wildly around the interior of the car, swooping into the front windshield with a dull thud, then the back, oblivious to the benevolent nature of my attempts to shoo her out.

I rolled down all the windows thinking she would feel the night air and head toward it, but she had chosen her route to freedom and it was through tempered glass. Back and forth she flew, bouncing between the windshields. If it was possible to feel more helpless than she, I did.

Resigned to her stubbornness, I pulled away from the mailbox, down the driveway and into the carport, wondering if I'd have to leave the windows down all night to induce her exit. My cheek was still stinging from its buffing by bird wing.

I stopped the car and stepped out and, just as I did, I heard a thud—Mama bird had found her way out of the car and was now flying herself repeatedly into the ceiling of the carport. "Please, little bird," I heard myself pleading out loud, "fly into the open."

And she did. Finally.

And I went inside, turned off the porch light, and leaned against the wall to catch my breath.

We're all birds. We live life simply and without much thought until we end up trapped by our responses to unexpected events. We think we see the way out of our prisons and, rather than listen to the voices that are trying to show us the way, end up bruised and frightened from throwing ourselves, over and over again, against invisible walls.

Somewhere, probably back in the mailbox nest, the bird slept with her head tucked against her chest. I slept with the rhythm of her wings still pulsing in my cheek.

APRIL 9, 2006

Before this morning, the last time I'd looked outside my office window was several weeks ago. At that point the gingko tree looked a lot like a skinny piece of coral in the bottom of somebody's fish tank. Rough and naked, branches sticking out at odd angles, the thousands of buds with aspirations of being fluttery dancing leaves someday were nothing more than so many ugly thumbs, short and fat and ugly.

Today those buds are gone, exploded into tiny trumpet-shaped leaves the color of the season's first pears. They fidget nervously in the morning breeze like children waiting for the school bus. The thin branches curve up and down, a hand beckoning me out into the sunshine.

How, I wonder, did I miss the change? How did I, a woman who would describe herself as attentive and thoughtful, let spring arrive unnoticed? What unimportant tasks on my endless to-do list kept me cumbered about with so much serving that I missed the better part?

I am tempted to offer up a defense. I do, after all, have to work for a living. And there is a house to maintain and social obligations to meet and infrequent distractions like doctors' appointments. And to minimize the need for those doctors' appointments there's the gym. And...

The truth is that my defense, any defense, would have a hard time standing up to the fact that all I had to do was turn my head. Turn my head away from the computer screen, away from the desk, away from the telephone for a matter of ten seconds. Turn my head all of ninety degrees. Just turn my head.

When I was about five years old, Mama left me in the car in the parking lot of the Simmons Shopping Center to run into McConnell's for a spool of thread or a zipper or a pack of hemming tape, some sewing notion. It was, in the 1960s, perfectly safe to do that. There was no chance of my being abducted nor of Mama being reported to DFCS.

She wasn't in the store very long, but as she was coming out she ran into someone she knew and stopped to chat. She could see the car and me in it and I could see her.

For some reason that I don't remember I decided to disobey Mama's specific instructions to stay where I was. I got out of the car and ran toward where she was standing on the sidewalk in front of the store.

I didn't see the car. But I heard it. Tires screeching, rubber desperately trying to grip the asphalt. And I heard Mama scream. I have absolutely no recollection of what happened after she ran into the street and grabbed me.

It was at that moment that I learned the concept of danger. It is my first memory of being afraid. I had tried to cross a street without looking, without turning my head, and it nearly killed me.

You would think that a lesson like that would stay with you forever. That you'd learn to live without blinders. That you'd learn, for goodness sake, to turn your head every once in a while. To see what lingers or lurks in the periphery.

You would think so. Until you remembered how easy it is to concentrate on the immediate to the exclusion of the yet-to-come or, to use John Covey's terms, the urgent over the important.

There have been plenty of times when, had I taken just a brief glance to my right or to my left, I'd have made a better decision, avoided some difficulty, had more fun. Plenty of times. Too many times.

The gingko tree buds swelled and opened and metamorphosed into gingko tree leaves and I missed it. And I missed it because I forgot, if only for a while, the danger that always exists when I become so focused on what is right in front of me that I neglect to turn my head.

APRIL 23, 2006

She came early. And though at nearly seven pounds she bears little resemblance to the tiny ones with which we've become familiar through the gravely-narrated documentaries on The Discovery Channel, she is not yet ready for the world.

The first pictures show lots of tubes held in place by wide white tape. There is a monitor of some kind attached to a tiny finger no bigger than a drinking straw and its red flourescent light makes her look like an infant E.T..

She is eight hundred miles away and the thoughts of her struggling for breath, of her mama and daddy pacing unfamiliar hallways, of her big brother not understanding why he cannot see the sister he has so eagerly awaited create a deep chasm in my chest. My shoulders fold in on each other as though they could shield my heart from the hurt.

I am thinking of her, of them all, as I walk down the road with Lily and Tamar. They have wandered off into the woods on the trail of something fascinating and the only sound is the padding of my feet on dry dry dirt. In this place where quiet and solitude so often provide respite and comfort, this day they offer only an empty place where the frustration of powerlessness wraps around me like a too-big overcoat.

Her mother and I had a conversation once about how our lives had connected, how it seemed we'd unwittingly bought tickets for the same train, a train that barreled across the countryside at unreasonable speeds in an unknown direction with nary an opportunity for us to change our minds and get off.

I remember that conversation now, on this late afternoon in April while so far away she sleeps under the bright lights of a hospital neonatal intensive care unit. Wonder if any of us on the train ever considered the possibility that the track would veer off in this direction.

When I was ten or twelve I rode my first roller coaster, the Dahlonega Mine Train at Six Flags over Georgia. I didn't know what to expect and so, of course, was not afraid. I shared the car with Daddy and held on to the heavy metal bar in front of us so tightly that when the ride was over I had flakes of rusty red paint on my hands. The abrupt swinging from side to side, the sudden drops coming on the heels of the creaking climbs, the involuntary screams I heard coming from my open mouth left me with the unassailable knowledge that I did not want to do that again.

And yet I did. The daughters in the family traveling with us, both younger than I, insisted that we ride again, this time sans parents. The second time I was afraid. I had been through it before and knew what was coming. With every turn I visualized the car flying off the track into the tops of the trees. It was horrible.

I was too young to know anything about physics or kinetic energy or to understand that we don't always get the chance to choose who or what we trust.

As my feet carry me up the road toward the sunset, I find myself thinking that the train the new one's mama and I are riding, that we are all riding, is not a whole lot different from a roller coaster. There is a reason there are no stops, no chances to get off, no opportunities to avoid the anxious ascents and precipitous plunges. And that reason, of course, is this: given the chance, we would get off.

If we were handed a detailed map as we walked up the steps or offered virtual reality goggles at the ticket window no one would ever leave the station. If all the possible hazards and the statistical likelihood of their appearance were announced by the conductor none of our trips would ever take us farther than the next curve in the road. If we knew ahead of time how hard would be the journey most of us would choose to stay home.

And by doing so we would miss the exquisite thrill that is a life well lived.

Life cannot be scripted; the journey cannot be planned and executed like a bus tour with sights of interest and comfortable overnight accommodations. Many days we end up with rusty red paint on our hands or high-tech monitors attached to our fingers.

On those days all we can do is trust the laws of physics and congratulate ourselves for hanging on.

MAY 7, 2006

First blackberries. First taste of the taste I've tasted every summer for as long as I can remember. Taste of earth and sunshine. Liquid tartness. Memories of bare feet on hot sand and suntanned arms covered in scratches. Mothers cautioning, cousins laughing.

It is still April when I spy the bumpy red berries drooping from the vines along the ditches. Make a note, I tell myself. In a couple of days the red will be black-purple, the bumps will be soft and full of juice. Just a couple of days.

I am right. When I come back two days later, it takes but a minute or two to scavenge up a handful. I call to the dogs, show off my treasure.

I take a deep breath and the scent of honeysuckle fills me. The white and yellow trumpets are everywhere. They hang from branches like lithe and limber trapeze artists. They poke through the holes in rusted-out fence rows and wrap themselves around the four-way stop sign like an over-possessive lover.

The road is trimmed in animal tracks: the wide ric-rac swathe of a gopher tortoise, the narrower rope twist cording of a snake of uncertain venom, the tight pinprick smocking of a covey of quail. Everything moves when the days grow long and mild.

The pine trees on either side of the road reach toward each other. Their branches don't quite meet, a perfect cathedral arch broken in the middle, a frame for a sky that is baby-blanket blue. The breeze that catches a curl and blows it into my eyes is warm like a towel just out of the dryer.

The poet e.e. cummings called spring "mud-luscious" and "puddle-wonderful." He lived in a darker, damper climate. My spring, our spring, the spring of the coastal plain is breezy and sunny and dry with just enough water to thrust the shiny green sword-blades of corn through the crisp gray veil of topsoil, just enough water to settle the dust that flies up behind the tires of pickup trucks rattling their way over field roads and pond dams.

My spring, our spring is less a party than a respite, a way-station between gray and somber winter and hot and weary summer. In spring we pause to catch our breath.

I eat the blackberries one by one. Later, when the vines are heavy, spilling over, dragging the ground, I will pick and pick and eat them by the handfuls. I will crowd my mouth with juicy sweetness, have my fill of perfect ripeness and still have enough left in the Tupperware container to make a cobbler (just flour and sugar and butter and berries) for supper. But that will be later.

Today is the day for first blackberries. Today it is important to savor, to relish, to delight in the single berry. To make the handful last at least as far as the top of the hill where I remember there are other bushes, where there lies the magical possibility of more.

Today is the day. Today it is important to savor, to relish, to delight in the single day, the single moment. To make it last. To understand that, along with the magical possibility of more, there also lies at the top of the hill or around the corner the possibility of less, of loss.

The last one. I hold it between my thumb and index finger. It is the fattest one, the deepest purple. I have saved it for last intentionally. I open my lips, drop it into my mouth. The flavor spreads over my tongue. Is that a seed or sand caught between my teeth? It doesn't matter. I have tasted spring.

MAY 21, 2006

A few weeks ago a tugboat on its way to New York found a loggerhead sea turtle floating off the coast of Georgia. A mature male weighing somewhere around five hundred pounds, his shell had been cracked by an apparent brush with a boat and, as a result, filled with gas preventing him from sinking and swimming underwater. The men on the boat somehow got him aboard and delivered him to the Department of Natural Resources office in Brunswick.

My friend Lea works at DNR and took the picture that made its way into the Brunswick newspaper and elsewhere. Attaching the picture to an e-mail, she explained how rare it is to see a live mature male and described looking into his face and seeing "very wise eyes." "Simply amazing," she wrote. "I have never seen anything like it."

Neither had I. Staring at the close-up shot of the turtle's face the first thing I noticed, though, was the barnacles. Everywhere. Whole sections of his face covered in the hard spiky knobs. Some as big as pie plates. Others as small as buttons.

My first reaction was disgust. They reminded me of scabs, of oozing wounds, of irritating blisters that cry out to be popped. My inclination was to grab a knife or a letter opener and start prying them away. I wanted to clean him up, make him comfortable, free him from his parasitic houseguests.

But then I, too, noticed his eyes. Large and deep-set. Dark with the secrets of the ocean. Moist and reflective. What had he seen? What did he see now? I had a feeling that if I stared into them long enough I would learn something, something important, something that would answer significant questions, something that would satisfy a longing I couldn't identify but felt intensely.

I looked away from the photograph and stared out the window a moment to re-center myself in reality. What was it about this turtle, this animal that captured me? Why did this creature who had spent his entire life in the ocean seem so familiar? Why did he seem to me, to Lea, to—I suspect—everyone who had seen him so venerable, so wise?

Certainly the loggerheads have no such reputation. One of the reasons their populations have dwindled over the past few decades is their gullibility. Hatched in beach nesting areas, the hatchlings instinctually head for the light along the horizon that is reflected off the surface of the ocean. Disoriented by the inland lights of civilization they can turn toward land rather than out to sea. Those that do make it into the water often die from eating balloons and plastic bags that they mistake for jellyfish.

I took another look at the picture. Stared at him so closely that I no longer saw the ugliness of the barnacles, only the beauty of stillness and rest and surrender.

And, suddenly, I recognized the wisdom. Mortally injured and absolutely helpless, he did not struggle. All his strength leached out by days and days in a wide lonely ocean, he floated. His nature was to dive, to swim, to search for food, but his encounter with man had left him without the ability to do what came naturally. Without a choice, he let go.

Once he let go, the currents pushed him toward the shore where man, the cause of his distress, arrived to save him. Ironic. But, then, life always is.

JUNE 4, 2006

The secret to citronella candles is this: You have to light them long before you want them to work.

I made this amazing discovery just last night when I decided to enjoy a cricket and bullfrog concert from Sandhill's new deck. Previous attempts to repel buzzing critters with citronella had been patently unsuccessful, but this candle came in a cute wire lantern and I had paid something like twenty dollars for it, so I figured I had to at least try.

Distracted by a telephone call from a friend who lives all the way across the state and who is as talkative as I, it was an hour or so later when I went back outside to find that the only thing hovering around my lounge chair was the smell of citronella. No mosquitoes. No gnats. No moths.

Obviously, I determined, the effectiveness of citronella is not immediate. In order to operate at optimum efficacy, the oil must be dispersed over a period of time. I was delighted. More than delighted. Ecstatic. More than ecstatic. Can a person be more than ecstatic over something like citronella?

It might be argued that my interlude on the deck does not hold the same significance as, say, the bubble bath taken by Archimedes that resulted in his discovery of the principles of buoyancy and density, but my response was much the same as his: "Eureka!" (Though for the sake of my reputation I must add that I did not go running down the dirt road naked.)

Free from the necessity of swatting and slapping, I stretched out and listened to the croaking and chirping, the occasional slap of some night bird's wings. I felt the breeze on my bare arms, watched the flame of the candle flutter like a ribbon in the wind. I let my muscles relax, lifted my hair up off my neck and took a deep breath. I leaned back and looked up at the stars, pinpricks of white light in a black sky.

This farm, this house, this deck, this me—we were all, suddenly, very very small.

These fields, this branch, these fence rows have been my home for more than thirty years. When Daddy moved us out here, I was a teenager who was constantly looking ahead. Today was to be endured, tomorrow hurried toward. I knew a lot of words, but I didn't know a morning glory from a blazing star. I had read a lot of books, but I'd never seen an armadillo or a red-cockaded woodpecker. Rain was an inconvenience, stillness something to be avoided at all costs.

Sitting here in the quiet, it is hard to remember that girl. If I met her now, I would be gentle with her ignorance, patient with her impatience. I would remind myself that she is only a bud, that she will open, change shape, have a fragrance all her own.

I would not reprimand her for the vision she has of herself as large and important and, oh, so independent. There is, I would tell myself, plenty of time ahead for her to learn how good it is, every once in a while, to feel small. And needy.

I would smile at her and know that she will eventually learn that it is when we recognize our connection to all things, when we surrender ourselves to the knowledge of need that mysteries are solved, riddles are answered, secrets are revealed.

Like the secret to citronella candles, which, incidentally, is also the secret to a lot of other things. Things like charcoal briquets. Metal halide lights. A child's curiosity. And love.

JUNE 18, 2006

It had not rained that day. And, yet, there was a rainbow.

I was walking down the beach at St. Simons, chatting with a friend I'd happened to meet as I parked my car at the old Coast Guard Station. The conversation was light. We were catching up, the pace of our walking and our chatting rapid and clipped. In the middle of a sentence she stopped and pointed. "A rainbow. No, wait, a double rainbow."

I turned toward the ocean and tilted my head back. Stretching out over the water from the beach on Jekyll was a pale wash of colors, colors like a nursery, like tropical fruit, like your first set of watercolors. The curve reached up into the billowy white clouds in a perfect arc, etched by a gigantic compass.

Like little children seeing the wonder for the first time, we stopped our talking to stand and stare. I could feel the sand warming my feet, the afternoon breeze raising the hairs on my bare arms. The landscape seemed to dissolve into one still frame. A double rainbow. Does that make the promise doubly secure?

On the other side of the cloud bank the rainbow appeared again, bending down toward Sea Island where the more expensive homes are built, where they had to put up a gate after its beauty was marred and its security destroyed by violence. But this was a single rainbow. Its twin had somehow disappeared.

Wallace Stegner—American writer, teacher of writers, environmentalist—once wrote, "No place is a place until things have happened in it." At the risk of being disrespectful, I would embellish his thought and suggest that no place is a place to you until things have happened in it to you.

I have lots of such places. There is the farm where I live, where I watch the seasons circle and spin. And Wesleyan, where I met and learned to like myself. And Dahlonega, where I spent three summers working at the hardest—but clearly the best —job I ever had. There is Highlands, where friends have sheltered me and taught me the song of waterfalls. There is Lake Blackshear and Forsyth Park and a blueberry farm outside Nahunta.

And there is St. Simons. What Marjorie Kinnan Rawlings, another writer and environmentalist, would call my "little place of enchantment," the place to which I am drawn by some undefined but clearly recognized magnetic force. The place where I fell in love with the ocean. The place to which I have, more times than I can remember, run away to breathe in the salt air and clear my mind. The place that never ceases to welcome me with broad marsh arms as I drive over the causeway.

A place where things have happened.

I looked up at the broken rainbow, its beauty somehow enhanced by its brokenness, its sudden singularity. It had soared into the clouds a pair and fallen back to earth alone, but its colors were still luminous, still recognizable. It was still a rainbow and, I suspected, still led to a pot of gold.

A couple of deep breaths, more like sighs really, and my friend and I continued down the beach. The conversation picked back up. We talked of next week and next month. We laughed at something silly. We turned and headed back.

I have never been able to watch a rainbow until it fades. It seems a bit voyeuristic. Somewhere between the King and Prince and the boatyard this one vanished. As I got back in the car and brushed the sand from my feet I noticed for the first time that it was gone. And I recognized once again that my island is a place, for something had happened here.

JULY 2, 2006

It started in October, what I refer to as The Great Sandhill Facelift, and—God willing and the rates don't rise—it will be finished in a couple of weeks. All I can say is Hallelujah!

Sandhill was built fifteen years ago and she was showing some age. The hurricanes of 2004 that brought rain and rain and more rain advanced that age significantly. I looked at the water stains running down the living room wall and the crumbling ceiling in the guest room and decided that as long as the place was going to become a construction zone I might as well do a little cosmetic work at the same time.

Eight months later I am a more patient woman. I am also wiser.

This is what I've learned:

1. The difficulty in making choices is having too many options. Walking into a hardware store to choose one doorknob from twelve different, but only slightly different, doorknobs can be overwhelming. Choosing one doorknob from three is much easier.

2. Construction projects do not involve problems. Cancer is a problem. Global warming is a problem. Juvenile delinquency is a problem. Someone stepping through the ceiling while working in the attic is not a problem. It is an irritation. A delay. Perhaps even, one day in the future, a joke.

3. Dust happens. Grinding and cutting anything, be it wood or stone or drywall, produces dust and dust will find its way into books and picture frames, under cabinet doors and rugs, through clothes. Try not to breathe too deeply.

4. Improvisation is not optional. When the tile man has to leave the toilet in the shower for five days, you pick up your makeup and move to the other bathroom. When the new door has a hole for a dead bolt where the old door didn't and the dead bolt

hasn't arrived yet, you stuff a dish towel in the hole and hope the power bill doesn't double.

5. Preparation isn't fun, but there's no avoiding it. Taking the legs off the dining room table and moving it piece by piece into the bedroom isn't a fun way to spend a Sunday afternoon. Neither is emptying closets and leaving piles of clothes in the middle of the floor for three days, but I had to do my part before the painters, the floor installers, the plumbers could do theirs.

6. If you can imagine it, it can be built. You may not have the materials to build it, but there is someone who does. You may not understand the mechanics of building it, but there is someone who does. You may not even know someone who has the materials and understands the mechanics, but there is someone who does. All you have to do is find him.

7. The only thing that can't be changed is the foundation. You can be fickle about flooring, capricious about color. Walls and windows can be moved, electrical lines re-run, roof lines altered. But not the foundation. That footprint determines what the house will become, all it will ever be. Burned down, torn down, fallen down years later, all that will be left of the shelter and sanctuary is the foundation. Which is why one must be careful in how it is laid.

I was sharing with someone not long ago the long list of changes and improvements at Sandhill—the deck, new roof, new floors and countertops, new furniture. "Sounds like a whole new house," she said.

"No," I assured her. "She's the same girl. She just has on a new dress."

Now that I think about it, I may not have been talking just about the house. I may have been talking about myself as well. Some changes, like new furniture, we make voluntarily. Others, like a new roof, are thrust upon us by storms that sweep across the landscape unannounced. Either way, it's important to remember one more thing I've learned:

Perspective is essential. Paying too much attention to picking out paint colors may leave the hummingbird feeder empty and the petunias dead. It can also leave a person too invested in what is, despite the length of a thirty-year mortgage, just a temporary abode.

JULY 16, 2006

When I turned on my cell phone the other morning, that nice lady with the soothing voice told me I had a new message. I was a little surprised; I rarely get any calls between ten o'clock at night when I turn the phone off and seven o'clock in the morning when I usually turn it back on.

After pressing all the right keys and entering my security code I got a brief message from Lauren confirming that a package I'd sent had been received. That's good. Except that the nice lady came back on and said the message was from June 30 at 12:12 p.m. and it was now July 9 at 9:00 a.m. Between the time Lauren called and the time I got her message we'd talked a couple of times and actually seen each other for several hours at a social engagement.

For almost nine days the message had been ... where?

It's my opinion that the world has two kinds of people: scientists and poets. The scientists are those whose thought processes require a logical, rational, provable explanation for everything. They tend to denigrate emotion and elevate analysis as a basis for decision making. They take the scientific method outside the laboratory and apply it to their relationships, requiring observable, empirical, measurable evidence before accepting anything. And, in fact, rarely do they accept anything as fact. It's all just theory.

On the other hand, there are the poets. The people who believe in magic. The people who can stand on a beach and look at a full moon and watch the tide going out, feeling the edges of their bodily selves melt away, becoming part of the rhythm without any need to understand anything about tidal physics. The people who—as William Blake put it—"see the world in a grain of sand."

I have no idea how the scientists would answer my question about where my message had been for those nine days since I am not, I suppose it is obvious, a scientist. I would guess that they would offer some explanation involving the word "cyberspace," defined, as I learned from looking it up on Wikipedia, as "a metaphoric abstraction used in philosophy and computing ... which represents the Noosphere/Popperian cosmology ... both 'inside' computers and 'on' computer networks." Say what?

Cyberspace is not a real space, a longitudinal and latitudinal dot on the globe, a place with an address, a location on the map. It's not even a spot in the sky, a point of light we can turn into the handle of a dipper or the tip of a hunter's arrow. We talk about it that way because it is an idea so hard to conceptualize that we've all—scientists as well as poets—just decided, like the Emperor's courtiers, to pretend we understand it when we don't.

Which brings me back to magic. Sitting out on the deck in the early morning sun, thinking about my friend's voice waiting somewhere for nine days for me to hear it, a hummingbird appeared. He hovered about two feet in front of my face, tiny little wings flapping so rapidly as to appear as nothing more than a blur and sounding a lot like the motor in my computer when I turn it on first thing in the morning. The iridescent green on his back caught the light like an emerald, its facets shooting off in all different directions. His beak, so perfectly shaped for poking into the face of a flower and purloining nectar, pointed straight at me. His eyes watched me closely in momentary surveillance. And, then, he was gone.

That, I decided, is what happens when we send our voices over telephone lines or bouncing between satellites. We free them to become hummingbirds. They fly, they hum, they hover. And eventually they come to rest.

It's not an explanation that would satisfy the scientists, and, quite frankly, the next time that cell phone dies for some inexplicable reason I'll be looking for one of those scientists to figure out what happened and fix it. It is an explanation, however, that satisfies me. I'm a poet. And I believe in magic.

JULY 30, 2006

There were nine of us around the table. We laughed. We cried. We told stories. We told secrets. We looked for all the world exactly like the girls we had been at seventeen.

Except we weren't.

I'm not exactly sure whose idea it was for all of us to get together for a joint birthday party, a celebration of the year in which we would all turn fifty, but once it was proposed it seemed the perfectly obvious thing to do. So we all showed up with our covered dishes (Was I the only one wondering when we turned into women who make covered dishes?) in our subtly accessorized outfits and warmed up to each other by passing around photographs of children, grown and near-grown.

It could have been a supper club or a baby shower or Tupperware party at any home in any subdivision in any town in the South. There were congratulations extended to the grandmother-to-be, condolences to the one whose father had died in the spring, introductions of the daughter who wandered through the house in all her effortless long-legged beauty. Ever the gracious ladies, we took turns reporting on the current states of our lives, allowing for well-mannered interruptions inserted like the detailed footnotes Miss Brannen required in our senior English term papers.

And at just the right moment our hostess suggested that we eat. Fill our plates with casserole and congealed salad. Gather at the table, elbow to elbow, and let the grace that was said rise up and fall down on our heads like a baptismal sprinkle.

What is it about a table that pulls us toward a center like a drawstring tightens an apron?

The volume went down. The words came slower. The camouflage of toothy grins relaxed into peaceful smiles. The stories got longer and deeper and truer.

I watched the faces of my friends, women who with whom I had learned to read, with whom I had stood in front of the old

Piggly Wiggly and sold Girl Scout Cookies, with whom I had decorated parade floats and sold yearbook ads and dissected frogs. I watched those beautiful faces—even more beautiful than they had been at seventeen—and saw not the crinkles at the corners of their eyes, but the light in their eyes.

I sat next to one of the teachers. Now holding three degrees, she didn't earn the first one until she was thirty-seven and already a wife and mother. Across the table sat another who had gone with her husband and two small children to serve as missionaries in Africa for two years and later lived through the trauma of breast cancer, the same disease that had taken her mother when she was the age we were celebrating.

Someone began singing the song we'd learned in Brownies: "Make new friends but keep the old. One is silver and the other gold." We all joined in.

I wanted to gather each of them into my arms, kiss her on the forehead and tell her how precious she is, how brave and strong and lovely she is, how right it is that we remind each other of who we were before we became who we are.

It was late when we finished the birthday cake—a decadent cheesecake whose one candle was jointly extinguished after we'd sung "Happy Birthday To Us." I drove home in the warm summer midnight and in my imagination lined up each of those girls in front of the woman she had become.

The captain of the cheerleaders had become the wife of a football coach. The pianist among us had become the wife of a singer. Two had married the boys who'd taken them to prom. All but three had become teachers. Beyond those predictable or at least not surprising outcomes, however, were the circuitous and unexpected routes that had somehow led us back, for a few hours on one summer night, to a common table.

T.S. Eliot reminds us that "the end of all our exploring will be to arrive where we started and know the place for the first time." That is, to hold in our hands both silver and gold.

AUGUST 13, 2006

All the lights are off. From the branch behind the house, a Greek chorus of crickets and frogs chants summer's song. The stifling heat of the day has settled into a halo of dampness floating over my bare arms and legs.

Standing on the deck, damp itself from the late afternoon thunderstorms that flattened the petunias in the hanging baskets, I look up at the moon. Full and ripe, it feels near enough to touch. And if I were able to touch it, I would feel its pulse, the rhythm that strokes the coastlines of the world with the tides, high and low, ebb and flow.

One of the folkloric names for the August full moon is the Green Corn Moon. In the darkness I cannot see the cornfields that rim two sides of Sandhill, but I know that they are far from green. Dry and brittle, the fragile fronds rustle in the breeze, their song a lament to a hot and dry summer.

Earlier this week I was walking back to the house just after sundown when a slight breeze picked up. I heard it before I felt it; the dead and dying cornstalks rattled against each other like the dry bones in Ezekiel's valley, but there was no prophet to call them back to life.

I will never become accustomed to drought. Even after all these years of living on a farm, of watching the seasons at close range and with a serious financial interest, I cannot look at a field of blistered corn without feeling my heart clutch like a fist inside my chest. I have breathed in too much dust stirred up by tractor plows, watched too many crops shrivel in the heat, heard too many soft sighs of resignation come out of Daddy's mouth to view the dryness with anything less than grief.

I understand, though, that somewhere the corn is tall and straight and green as a gourd. Somewhere the water came when it was needed. Somewhere the clouds formed and emptied themselves on new blades just poking through the crust of soil. Somewhere, but not here.

I watch the moon for a while. It reminds me of an egg yolk, golden yellow orb floating in a thick black sky. It provides enough light, minutes before midnight, to distinguish colors, to perceive depth. It changes the night from a painting, a two-dimensional canvas, into a sculpture with sides and angles.

I turn to go back inside and notice the other field that edges Sandhill, the one where peanuts are growing, lapping over in their double rows. The vines are dark and lush. The leaves are soft and bendable. The roots have pegged down into the dirt. The rain that came too late for the corn was just in time for the peanuts and in October the peanut plow will dig its spindly fingers into the ground and cup the vines toward the sun, an offering of thanksgiving for a hard-won harvest.

I am reminded of one of the earliest lessons I learned as a farmer's daughter: Some years are good; some are bad. Some bring enough rain, some too much, some not enough. Some crops make, some fail. The one who dares to predict is either a gambler or a farmer. Or both.

I take one last look at the moon. The full moon. The Green Corn Moon. There is someone up there. And I think I just saw him (or was it her?) wink.

AUGUST 27, 2006

It must have been in the first or second grade that we learned to make snowflakes. After explaining the unique nature of snowflakes—the "no two are exactly alike" speech—the teacher showed us how to take a sheet of white paper and fold and fold and fold, then take our blunt-end scissors and cut angles and arcs to make decorations for our classroom door.

My first attempt was timid. I was afraid of cutting away too much so I trimmed away thin slices and shallow slivers. When I unfolded it all I had was a piece of white paper with a few holes in it, nothing like the delicate lacy creations that our teacher had made.

After wadding up any number of sheets of vandalized paper and subtly surveilling the other students at my table, I garnered enough courage to attack my paper with long slashes and deep incisions. The resulting snowflake was breathtaking, to me if to no one else.

I was in a lovely art gallery in Chattanooga last weekend. There were beautiful bronze sculptures of wrinkled faces. There were hand-woven wall hangings and mixed-media collages. Blown glass vases and carved wooden toys shared display cases with jewelry made from antique silver. The walls were covered in canvases painted in rich colors and prints that were astonishingly deep in their muted tones.

It is a gift to see beauty where others do not. It is talent to see in one's mind what does not exist and use one's hands to bring it into existence. It is genius that makes intangible tangible. The rooms of the gallery were filled with genius. And, with my arrival, a little bit of envy.

Back home, I was reminded of beauty and snowflakes and genius the next morning when I woke up to find a long, loopy swag etched into the condensation on the doors to the deck. Perfectly centered on the glass, it looked as though someone had stenciled it there in the night. Intrigued at how the design had gotten there, I stared closely.

There are no trees or bushes close enough to have swayed in the wind and drawn the pattern. I'd heard no bird bang into the glass and madly beat his wings against the panes. These were not handprints or fingerprints.

I laughed out loud when I realized that the artist had been a tree frog. Back legs splayed wide and front feet spread to show off what amounts to knobby fingers, the frog had moved from one side of the doors to the other in a compass-perfect arc. He hadn't intended to create something of beauty, of course. He was just trying to get to someplace drier than the ground that had been saturated with late summer rain. But he did, just by being a frog and doing what a frog does.

Just as the river does by slowly polishing the stones that lie in its bed. Just as the moon does by spilling its reflected light onto the surface of the ocean. Just as the sun does by casting shadows, short then long then short again, across a wide front porch.

It was my friend Gena who noticed the ceramic creche in one of the display cases at the gallery. Glazed in pale rose and taupe, everyone—Mary, Joseph, the shepherds, even the animals—was looking skyward and everyone was wearing a smile. Something like the smile on my face when I made my first snowflake, when I applauded the tree frog. A smile like the one I am absolutely certain graced the face of the first artist when he looked about him and called his creation good and which reappears every time that creation responds in kind.

SEPTEMBER 10, 2006

Last summer I checked off one item on my "Things to Do Before I Die" list: I saw James Taylor in concert at Chastain Park in Atlanta. It is a delight to hear anyone make music under the stars at Chastain, and James Taylor could make the hairs on my arms stand up singing from a flatbed trailer in the Walmart parking lot. Somehow, though, I knew without knowing that that particular combination of artist and venue would be magic.

And it was.

The picnic supper that my friend Leesa and I packed wasn't nearly as elaborate as that of many of the other concert-goers. In fact, we didn't pack it at all; it came in white paper bags handed to us from the drive-through window at Wendy's, as I recall, but no foie gras, no candelabra, no expensive wine could have made the experience any better.

When James (pardon the familiarity, but we've been close for years) walked out onstage in faded jeans and a shirt with rolled-up sleeves, he was greeted with generous and genuine applause. When he dropped his head and began strumming the guitar there was a collective sigh. Every heart slowed a bit, every shoulder relaxed, the lines on every face smoothed out as though caressed by a mother.

He played and sang and made a few mild political jokes. He told the story of how "Sweet Baby James" had been written on his way to North Carolina to meet his brand new nephew, his namesake. He could get no farther than two bars into any given song before his knowledgeable audience began clapping its hands, first in recognition and then in rhythm.

The concert began at seven and it was very near eleven o'clock when he raised his long, lanky arm for a final wave and walked off, leaving us wanting more but not certain that we could contain a single note, or a single memory, more.

There is something about a guitar. More than any other musical instrument it draws you in, makes you a part of the music it creates. Perhaps it is because it is a relatively easy instrument to learn. Perhaps it is because so much popular music has been written for guitar. Perhaps it is because the pluck of the string is so very much like the pluck of one's heart.

A couple of friends came to Sandhill for a visit a week or so ago. It was the first night in weeks that the heat had lifted enough at nightfall that we could sit outside and enjoy the feel of late summer. The air was thick and warm. Martins appeared from the branch and dive-bombed bugs that only they could see. Fireflies mimicked the starlight in the navy blue sky.

One of my friends walked inside for a moment and returned exclaiming, "Look what I found!" He had in his hands my old guitar. It hadn't been played by anyone in over three years. "You mind if I play?"

"Not at all," I told him, "if you can tune it."

"He can tune it," his wife said in the voice of the long-married and still-enamored, a voice one doesn't hear so often these days.

And he did. In just a few minutes recognizable chords were pulsing out from his fingers. In a couple more he was singing and, then, without really noticing it, I was singing with him. Song after song. A couple of verses of this one, a chorus or two of another, one entire ballad about some poor soul who'd gotten stuck on the trolley in Boston because he didn't have the fare to get off.

We sat there, the three of us and the guitar, making music and memories until the dew was a near-puddle on the top of the table and our voices near-whispers in the darkness. Then we went inside and locked the doors, the music still floating in the air.

There is something about a guitar. And a summer night. And hearts that are willing to sing.

SEPTEMBER 24, 2006

Every once in a while I make what I call a whirlwind tour of the metro area. The tour involves my driving up to Atlanta where a significant number of people I love happen to live and trying to see as many of them as possible within a forty-eight-hour (plus or minus) period.

Just last weekend I orchestrated such a trip. I created a table on my computer and made columns for the date, the time, the person and the location. I filled in the grid as people confirmed our appointments and, just before I left, I printed it out and put it in a folder with MapQuest directions to the various locations to which I'd be going. Loaded down with hostess, housewarming, birthday, and shower gifts, I hit the road. And before I got home Sunday night I'd managed to see thirteen friends.

(Note: According to a quote published just recently in the local newspaper, "A neurosis is a secret that you don't know you are keeping." I would posit, therefore, that having shared and thereby acknowledged my behavior, I cannot be considered neurotic and any questions as to my sanity should be forestalled until further notice.)

I have always said that I have the best friends in the world. They are, by and large, an eclectic bunch and as my weekend junket progressed I was even more convinced of that. We talked, we laughed, we cried, we ate. We talked some more.

And I learned some things. Particularly from the friend who on Sunday morning met me for a breakfast that turned out to be every bit as enlightening and inspiring as if we'd been inside a church instead of outside a coffee shop on Peachtree Street.

It's not been an easy year or so for my friend. The youngest of four children and the only one who'd lived nearby, she'd carried most of the responsibility for the care of her aging and ailing mother. After her mother died she was left to oversee the dissembling of a home that had nurtured three generations.

When we made arrangements to meet she told me that she had just returned from that home, from loading the last of the boxes, labeling the last of the furniture, and that she'd be returning on Monday to close the sale of that home.

"Are you okay?" I had asked with the hesitation that always colors a question whose answer may or may not be comfortable.

"I am," she said with only the slightest tremble in her words. "Mama always said, 'Don't cry over anything that can't cry over you.'"

Nibbling on our low-fat cranberry-orange scones in the Sunday morning light of a city that never goes dark, the conversation included a lot of sentences that started with "Mama always said" or "Mama always told me." A portrait of a funny, unconventional woman appeared. A portrait that looked remarkably like the daughter who had been my friend for thirty years.

Nothing, however, struck me with the force of that first comment: Don't cry over anything that can't cry over you.

Driving back down the interstate on my way home I thought about the things I'd cried over and, the truth is, though I knew there were childhood disappointments and teenage crises and even adult stresses that had reduced me to tears, the only things I could remember were, in fact, the things that could cry over me.

And considering what every one of those things have brought into my life, I'd have to say that it's been worth every tear.

OCTOBER 8, 2006

October. The mustard and turnip patch has been planted. The broom sedge, which wasn't there two weeks ago, is beginning to grow along the edges of the fields and sways in the breeze that wasn't there two weeks ago either. The loosestrife is yielding to goldenrod. The hummingbirds have all but disappeared.

October. The sound of the school bus rattling over the washboard ridges in the road no longer startles as it did in late August. Deer, just beginning to darken with their winter coats, leap across that same road in long arcs leaving heart-shaped memos in the sand. The hues left behind in the sky as the sun falls quickly below the horizon are the colors of an old bruise, deep and dull.

October. Morning arrives in a gray-green mist that turns the farm into a magical landscape. I wouldn't be half surprised to see a wizard walk out of the branch and onto the porch to join me for breakfast. The chill in the air could be just temperature or it could be something more.

October is like the pumpkins that appear on every doorstep; it is full and round and seems to be just on the verge of exploding. Were the months of the year a house full of siblings, October would be the fourteen-year-old girl.

It is the fair and funnel cakes and a pancake supper. It is the World Series and football. It is trick or treat and self-inflicted scariness. It is also my birth month. And given the fact that this year is what we tend to consider a "big" birthday, I'm willing to concede that I may be just a little more attuned to the things that have always made October my favorite month.

Last night, just about dusk, I went walking with the dogs. October moments between sundown and hard dark spend more quickly than do the late afternoons of summer and, before I got too far, the moon, pushing the envelope toward full, was pouring silver-white light over the whole world.

The road leads through a tunnel of pine trees and the dogs running ahead were little more than shadows, dark and light. There were no animal sounds, no breeze to rustle the drying leaves or pine straw. My steps were soft and slow.

Suddenly, the moonlight fell over my shoulder in a bright white stream. Pouring through a break in the trees it looked like a huge floodlight, one of those on the tops of prison guard towers that scan the ground for escaping inmates. And that is exactly what I felt like—my back to the fence, razor wire hovering just over my head, blinded by the light, frozen by conspicuousness.

Turning back to the road, trying to refocus in the darkness, I couldn't help but wonder whether the metaphor had any significance. Do we, as the candles on the cake grow in number, blow them out with wistfulness and the desire to escape the lives we have? Or do we take a deep breath and exhale with a smile, perhaps even laughter, in contemplation of what lives we, with increasing wisdom and experience, are capable of creating?

As the darkness thickened and the details of the world blurred, I called out to the dogs the same command I always give them when it's time to turn for home, the command to which they always respond with speed and enthusiasm, the command they never question because they know they can trust me. "Let's go!"

And it was almost as if there was another voice, the voice of the young girl I used to be and the woman I was still to become, whispering the same thing to me. "Happy Birthday, Kathy. Now let's go!"

OCTOBER 29, 2006

At low tide—not on my beach, but another beach, one where the sand is less like confectioner's sugar and more like sandpaper—I went looking for, I thought, shells. But not exactly shells. Pieces of shells.

In our part of the world it is a rare occasion that presents a whole, unbroken, unblemished shell on the wet edge of the continent for someone to pick up and tote home, so I walked with my head bent, my eyes scanning the crunchy water line for interesting fragments.

Just a few strides from the boardwalk I found half a sand dollar. It looked very little like the whole ones you find at seashell stores, the ones that are bleach-white and completely round, the ones whose five sets of pores on the top make a perfect Spirograph star. This fifty-cent piece of a sand dollar was exposing its inside, the cavity that in a living specimen is the water-vascular system that enables it to move, the cavity that—in death and dismemberment—was only an empty room.

I found more, smaller pieces as I walked. I picked them up, rattled them around in my palm. Pieces of a dollar. Quarters and dimes and nickels. Loose change. Not quite as easy to carry as a single bill, but still spendable.

Farther down the beach something glinted in the sand. I reached down to pick up a piece of moon shell. Smooth as glass, curved like a scythe, it was about the size of my thumbnail. I couldn't decide whether it was pink or brown or something in between. Either way, I thought and smiled at my vanity, it would make a pretty lipstick.

As I kept walking and scanning the water line it appeared that, in an effort to get my attention, the tide had deposited an embarrassment of moon shell pieces. Slivers, slices, chunks. All different, but all recognizable and all evocative of a full moon shell.

Just the night before I had stood and looked out over the ocean at a full moon. Its reflection in the water pulsed with energy, scattered illumination in all directions, outlined the landscape in softness like a filter on a camera lens. I had watched it and remembered other full moons, other nights standing under a shower of pewter light. I had stared at the pumpkin-colored ball poised in the sky at the exact point where its surface could be fully illuminated by the sun and thought of the mystery and magic we attribute to something that occurs only once every twenty-nine and a half days.

Why, I asked myself, holding the fragile pieces of moon shell in my hand, don't we see mystery and magic in the other days? Why do we reserve the awe and wonder for one night a month? Why do we save things—good china, linen napkins, our deepest emotions—for what we call "special occasions"?

The tide had turned, the roar of the waves had softened, and I could now hear in the rhythm of my footsteps the sound of thousands of shell fragments dissolving beneath my weight. Shells becoming sand.

Back over the dunes, through the sea oats, I carried my treasures: bits and pieces, parts and fragments, remnants and shards. I carried them with my palms turned up and open, the way I'd been told by a friend that one must carry anything of value.

It would be lovely someday to happen upon a seashell, whole and unbroken and unblemished. A pink and white conch or a tiger-striped chambered nautilus or a tightly spiraled whelk. But it is better still, I've decided, to look for loveliness in the pieces and parts and fragments that get scattered like crumbs along the shore.

Few dawns are heralded by full moons. Few shells survive the wash of the tide unbroken and unblemished. It is the other moons, new and waxing and waning, that usher in most mornings. It is the pieces of shells, worn down by the wash of water and broken by the weight of travelers, that form the beach. And it is the awe and wonder, the mystery and magic of the everyday, that is the currency of our lives.

NOVEMBER 12, 2006

Just the other day I was headed cross-country toward Valdosta—one of those places in our wide and wonderful state to which it is difficult to find a straight shot from here. Having gotten widely varying estimates of time and distance from three different Internet mapping services, I decided to play rabbit and head out in what I knew was the general direction, the back roads known as the Woodpecker Trail. I can't remember when I've enjoyed a drive more.

It was early Saturday morning. There were few other cars on the road so I could watch the landscape skim by. The yellow autumn light came through the trees at such an angle that the changing leaves all looked as though they'd been plated with precious metals. Acres and acres of cotton spread out on either side of the road and were so thick with fat fluffy blossoms that I couldn't help but hear the voices of my childhood preachers singing out from the pulpit about the fields being white with harvest.

Rounding a curve I saw a neatly painted sign dangling from a limb on a tall oak tree: Fresh Eggs - 1 mile. I was half-tempted to take the detour down the narrow dirt road just to meet the kind of folks who still sold eggs from their back porch.

At a county road crossroads, three shiny new pickup trucks, each one with a grill as big as a cattle gate, were parked on the gravel outside a cinder-block store. Men dressed in various degrees of camouflage leaned against the fenders, hands in pockets or crossed over their chests, soaking up sunshine and swearing to the number of points on the buck that had been just out of range.

I passed a sign that told me I'd entered the Big Hammock Wildlife Management Area, 7000 acres of floodplain habitat owned and managed by the state of Georgia. A few miles farther down the road I drove into Appling County and the road widened, took me over a new concrete bridge. Underneath ran the Altamaha River. It is the largest river of the Georgia coast and the second-largest river basin in the eastern United States. It flows for 140 miles through Southeast Georgia toward the Atlantic Ocean.

On this day the water was low, barely moving, and the sand looked like cake icing, creamy white and spread in gentle waves along the edges of the water. All was silence and stillness and I was suddenly struck with an instinctual protectiveness toward the river and all it represents. It was as though by being there at that particular moment I'd been vested with an ownership interest in that particular piece of creation.

I've experienced it before—at the foot of a waterfall in North Carolina, on the banks of a creek that runs along one edge of our farm, under an oak tree too big to circle with my arms, on top of the Temple Mound in Macon—and each time I've found myself breathless.

What is it, I wonder, about untouched nature that speaks so deeply to our souls? Do we hear our own breath in the wind? Feel our own pulse in the current?

There's been a lot of talk over the past thirty years or so about preserving our natural heritage and cleaning up the environment. We've spent a lot of money as a nation to do just that. And, yet, I'd bet that the majority of Americans don't see themselves as the owners, much less the caretakers, of a single square foot of dirt on which they are not paying a mortgage.

We have become so distanced from that which we didn't create that rain is just something that delays a baseball game and wind only something that interferes with the satellite signal. And 7000 acres of nothing but wetlands seems like a lot of wasted space.

Until you see it. Until you feel it. Until you own it for yourself.

NOVEMBER 26, 2006

A couple of months ago Lily and Tamar got into a terrible fight. It was Saturday night. We took them, in separate vehicles, to the animal emergency room, driving the twenty miles into town with all kinds of fear and trepidation that the vast amounts of blood spread all over Mama and Daddy's deck and laundry room were an indication of horrible, horrible injuries.

As it turned out, though they both had to stay the night, the only serious wound was one on Lily's left front leg that required stitches.

Once we got them home, we undertook a complex logistical effort to make sure that the two of them had no contact with each other. One got to play in the yard in the morning, the other in the afternoon. After years of sharing a bed, the two were banished to not just separate rooms, but separate houses. It was exhausting.

And emotionally draining. These two dogs have been bosom buddies for nearly six years. With the exception of four or five incidents involving bared teeth, otherworldly growling, and bites that drew blood, they were completely simpatico. They cried for each other when they were separated. They chased deer and rabbits and squirrels in tandem. They began each morning licking each other's faces as though to reassure themselves that all was right with the world.

When I took Lily back to Saint Buddy to get the stitches removed I asked him what we could do about the problem. He presented me with a copy of a scholarly article on "intraspecies female aggression" and warned me that what I was going to read would not make me happy.

He was right. The experts say that IFA, as I've come to call it, is not an unusual problem. There were explanations about canine society and the necessity of an alpha dog, warnings about trying to treat dogs equally as one would people and suggestions about behavior modification.

The experts' conclusion was that IFA is not easily solvable. In fact, they wrote, it is unlikely, once IFA has been introduced into the relationship, that the two dogs can ever be trusted with each other again.

It made me sad.

And it made me even sadder to think of the human application. It didn't take me long to thing of more than a handful of relationships, mine and other people's (and not limited to females, thank you very much), that had gone from close and loving and attached-at-the-hip to distant and cruel and vicious. And, like the veterinary experts said, most of those relationships cannot be healed.

With dogs the aggression is instinctual and arises from fear. We humans, with our advanced brains and social connections, are supposed to live beyond the reach of instinct, and yet it occurs to me that the source of all those broken relationships can in one way or another be traced back to fear. Fear of loss, fear of separation, fear of fear.

We're working with Lily and Tamar, carefully reintroducing them to each other. When I take Lily up to Mama and Daddy's each morning I hold her leash tightly and allow her and Tamar to touch noses through the wooden gate on the deck. We've even taken a couple of long walks, one on a leash, one loose, making sure that a safe distance between the two is maintained.

Neither one gets so much as a pat on the head until she responds to a command of, "Sit!"

Will it work? Will they somehow figure out the parameters of their relationship and learn the behavior that will allow them to once again run freely over hundreds of acres together? I don't know.

What I do know is that every time I look at them, separated by barriers that they created themselves, I see not just their faces, but human faces. And it makes me want to cry.

DECEMBER 10, 2006

It bothers me sometimes when I go to church and the preacher raps me on the head.

Not all the time. Sometimes the rap is a "Hello? Anybody home?" and it just wakes me up to something I already know but just hadn't considered in a while. And sometimes it's a "Hey! Guess what!" that makes me sit up straight and open my eyes a little wider.

But sometimes, every so often, when I'm sitting there in a column of sunshine slanting through the stained glass window on my pew, the preacher takes out a mallet—no, make that a meat tenderizer with all those spikes on it—and whacks me with a blow so sharp that it's hard not to yell "Ouch!" right there in front of God and everybody.

So I'm walking around this week with a big purple bruise underneath all this hair and still wondering why that one remark, not even a major point in the sermon, is still pulsing so hard and so regularly through whatever artery it is that connects the brain to the heart.

This is what he said: "The fear itself is a sign that God will keep His promise."

Say what? Isn't that a little, well, untheological? Isn't the whole idea of believing in God and ultimate eventual good supposed to produce something like spiritual endorphins? Isn't it supposed to leave us with, if only a platitude, at least a platitude when the Wicked Witch and all her flying monkeys surround us and our cowardly, ignorant, and heartless companions?

And especially on the first Sunday in Advent when we're supposed to be focusing on the promise of peace on earth and good will toward all of us and the angels are telling us to fear not, should those two things—promise and fear—really be riding on the same float in the Christmas parade?

Every year about this time I find myself pulling out my well-read copy of Barbara Brown Taylor's book of sermons, *Home By Another Way*. In the one she titled "Singing Ahead of Time," she talks about Mary, the teenager who managed somehow in what had to be the most frightening moment she'd ever experienced (but which would pale in comparison to the one she'd face about thirty-four years later) to believe, to take as truth a promise as yet unfulfilled. Taylor reminds us that Mary has no ultrasound, no DNA test identifying God as the father of her baby. "All she has," Taylor writes, "is her unreasonable willingness to believe that the God who has chosen her will be a part of whatever happens next."

Promise and fear. Together.

Promise belongs to the future, that unseen and untested place to which we would be drawn by our hearts even if our minds hadn't created it. And we are drawn to it even as we ask ourselves, trembling, "What if it isn't so?"

Joan of Arc. Christopher Columbus. Martin Luther King. Everyone who ever teetered on the edge of the high dive. Everyone who ever asked for a raise. Everyone who ever fell in love. Promise hand in hand with fear.

To be honest, I'm not sure that this particular stream of consciousness is what the preacher had in mind when he chose the lectionary reading from Luke as his text. Then again, it's not about what he had in mind when he entered the pulpit and it's certainly not about what I had in mind when I entered the pew.

It's about Christmas and the miraculous conception of not just a baby whose individual life would change every thought and idea and action that came after, but the conception of every thought and idea and action that would come after and change every life.

It's about, as Taylor put it, "singing ahead of time." Singing before there's a reason to sing. Believing the promise while feeling the fear. Standing between the two, holding out our hands, and becoming a bridge.

DECEMBER 24, 2006

It is not a perfect Christmas tree. Several of its branches dangle in slings made of fishing line to minimize gaping holes in its architecture. The lights are not exactly even. Some of the ornaments are faded and bent into something other than their original shapes. But it is, like Charlie Brown's tree, infused with a real-ness that arises from something other than lights and ornaments.

Dangling near the window and sending erratic flashes of light around the room is a tiny brass ornament with my name engraved along the bottom. My friend Pam's mother smoked Lord-knows-how-many-packs of Virginia Slims to redeem the personalized ornament offer for the six of us our freshman year at Wesleyan. On one of the lower, sturdier limbs is a three-dimensional representation of a runner lighting the Olympic torch, Sandra's acknowledgment in Christmas of 1996 of the great fun I had in being a part of the relay through Statesboro.

The mouse dressed as an angel was a gift from Jessica who sat at my conference room table one day and nearly lost her breath laughing at stories of my rodent phobia. The sea horse is made of St. Simons sand. The ceramic Claddagh reminds me of Mandy and Celtic music and all kinds of secrets.

Scattered over the limbs are the snowflakes and balls that Mama crocheted and the tiny Chrismons I cross-stitched when I got my first place. There is a glazed dough pig and a little balsa wood birdcage, a china bell painted with a dogwood blossom and a silver one engraved with my initials, a baseball that opens on a hinge to reveal Santa Claus in red and white pinstripes. A tiny porcelain cross hangs from a green ribbon near the top.

At the top of the tree is a big Waterford crystal star, a gift from Lucy and her parents the year we all stood in front of the judge whose hurried and harried attitude could not dampen our awe and delight at the legal acknowledgment of what we'd all known for some time—that Lucy was home.

There must be over a hundred ornaments on the tree, each one placed there by my hand, the touch connecting me to people and places and times, some of them gone forever except in my memory. It is not a perfect Christmas tree, but like every tree in every home in every town it is a representation of the life that is sheltered and nurtured here. It is, like the Little Prince's rose, unique in all the world.

Soon it will be taken apart, piece by piece, ornament by ornament, and packed away in the attic until next year. But on this Christmas Eve, between heading off to church in early morning to light the fourth Advent candle and heading back in the early darkness for Communion, I will still my thoughts and my heart long enough to sit and stare. To remember Pam's mother. To think about Sandra and Jessica and Mandy and Lucy. To say a prayer of gratitude for the hands that crocheted the snowflakes. To invite the spirits of all the people I love to join me under the tree in marveling at all we share.

JANUARY 21, 2007

Momofuku Ando has died. He was ninety-six. A Japanese entrepreneur, he was the founder of Nissin Food Products. He invented the instant noodle, what we call ramen noodles. What my college buddy Mona called, for no discernible reason, flexy noodles.

Ramen noodles were one of the staples of my law school diet, available at the Piggly Wiggly on Vineville Avenue for six packages for a dollar. I think I tried the shrimp flavor once, but most of the time I rotated among chicken, beef, and pork.

I wasn't much of a cook then, but standing over my tiny little apartment stove and watching the brittle square of noodles fall apart and soften in a pot of boiling water made me feel, somehow, a little more human. The steam would raise and swirl around my face and, after I opened the plastic-lined foil pouch and emptied the flavor packet into the pot, the scent of chicken soup would spread through my three tiny rooms like a cartoon genie freed from a magic lamp. It would creep into the curtains and the carpet and my winter coat draped over the back of one of the two chairs that bracketed my cinder-block-and-two-by-four bookshelves. The next day, when I came back from class and opened the door, the lingering aroma made those three rooms a little less empty.

Katherine was in graduate school at the same time I was in law school and her go-to meal (to use one of perky Rachael Ray's favorite phrases) was Kraft Macaroni and Cheese, only most of the time it wasn't Kraft but whatever generic brand the grocery store in Athens had on sale for three boxes for a dollar. She managed to get two meals out of a box, so she and I were pretty much on the same food budget.

At the time, of course, the idea of eating ramen noodles (or macaroni with powdered "cheese") three or four times a week wasn't as romantic as it appears in retrospect. More than once I had to remind myself that the economic deprivation of being a law student would not last forever, that one day I would be able to choose my meals based on something other than price. Over twenty-five years later, I can't remember the last time I bought a pack of ramen noodles. I haven't asked her, but I don't think Katherine has bought macaroni with fake cheese since her children were small.

The last time she and I ate together was a Christmas party at Sandhill. There was real china and crystal and flatware that I keep in a big wooden box. There were linen napkins and candles. And we ate real food, cooked from scratch. It was a lot of fun.

But, now that I think about it, not any more fun than the ramen noodles and mac and cheese days, the tiny apartment days, the our-whole-lives-before-us days. Days when there was nothing better than the free entertainment of standing on the Indian Mounds and watching the whole city spread out before us. Nights when there was nothing better than cruising down Highway 41 with the Guess Who wailing out "These Eyes" through the speakers on the 8-track tape player. Days and nights when there was nothing better than being young and eager and hungry.

The newspaper article that informed me of Mr. Ando's death said that the Chinese eat nearly 30 billion packs of ramen noodles each year and that 65.3 million packs were eaten worldwide in 2004. Mr. Ando died a very rich man. I hope he also died a happy man. I hope he knew that his noodles were more than just food for the body, that they were—in that odd backward glance kind of way—food for the soul.

FEBRUARY 4, 2007

"You need to come to Indianapolis," the voice on the other
end of the telephone announced with such assurance that it didn't
occur to me to question it. Barry is a salesman, a car salesman,
born to the breed. He is a hard person to contradict.

"You need to have some fun and I can promise you that we'll
give you some fun. So, when are you coming?"

I hesitated. Taken off guard, I mumbled a few words that
neither of us understood.

"You can't tell me no. I am not a person that someone can say
no to. You're going to come. You just tell me when."

"Let me check my calendar. I'll call you back."

Two weeks later Barry called me again. "You didn't call me
back," he said matter-of-factly. "So when are you coming?"

As I said, Barry is tenacious. And he loves his wife. Though
she is very happy in Indiana after living there for nearly sixteen
years, he recognizes that it can't hurt to continue to express his
gratitude for the fact that she packed up and left Georgia, two
toddlers in tow, to settle in a place where Easter outfits include
overcoats.

Barry also loves surprises and he had decided that my visit
would be a surprise. For three months we exchanged secret e-
mails and telephone calls and on the Thursday afternoon before
Martin Luther King Day, I found myself on a plane to Indianapolis
by way of Cincinnati (whose airport, incidentally, is not located in
Ohio, but Kentucky).

My plane from Savannah to Cincinnati was delayed an hour. I
called Barry. He was completely nonplused by the fact that his list
of lies about why he would be getting home late would now need
to grow by at least one. "I've got a plan," he told me and I
laughed. It's hard not to laugh at Barry.

I finally got to Indianapolis at ten o'clock. Barry and I hadn't
seen each other in fifteen years and I was wondering if we'd

recognize each other. I rounded the corner and there he was. His hair was grayer, mine was longer. Otherwise we looked about the same. It probably helped that at that hour the airport was virtually empty and there weren't that many passengers/people waiting from which the two of us had to choose.

"This is the plan," he told me. "I got an empty pizza box last night. I'm going to call Sandra and tell her that I'm ordering pizza. When we get home, I'll go inside and then you can go to the front door with the pizza box and ring the doorbell."

It went off without a hitch. One of those I-wish-I'd-had-a-camera moments. And the look on Sandra's face was worth the delay, worth the earache I always get as the plane descends, worth all of Barry's lies, for which he was immediately forgiven.

And I did have fun.

It didn't surprise me really, but time and distance have a way of eroding things and anyone with any amount of living behind her knows that not everything lasts.

Sandra and I met when we were ten years old. We have never lived in the same town. We have never spent more than five consecutive days in the same town. Except for the fact that we both love to talk better than just about anything, our personalities are near-polar opposites. Sandra is spontaneous; I am deliberate. Sandra is self-effacing; I am self-critical. Sandra is blonde; I am not. And yet somehow, over nearly forty years, we have remained friends. We have lasted.

What a comfort. What a joy. What a gift.

I read recently that golf balls originally had no dimples. They were perfect spheres, round and smooth. When a golfer made his swing, pulled the club back in an arc over his shoulder and brought it back down to hit the ball, the trajectory was more like a baseball line drive than a basketball floating jumper.

The story goes that only after a ball had been used for a while, whacked and beaten, scuffed and bruised, did it begin to take off, to lift into the air high above the heads of the golfers and caddies and spectators. It became obvious that the game was more interesting this way and in 1909 the Spalding Company began manufacturing balls with dimples, that is, imitation defects.

It is said that a dimpled golf ball will travel almost two and a half times farther than a smooth one.

Isn't that a great story? A morality tale that reminds us that being used over and over isn't always a negative thing. That paying attention to the way things work, rather than the way they are supposed to work, is the first step toward innovation. That it is sometimes the wounds we receive and the scars that remain that give us the loft to fly higher and farther.

I know some people who have been golf balls. People who rose to their greatest heights after having been beaten up a few times. And people who started their lives' journeys with all the right things—good family, intelligence, enough money—but who didn't accomplish much in the way of obtaining their hearts' desires until they'd been through some days when it seemed as though all the blinds in the world had been drawn shut and it would never be light again. And people who remembered that it was a game and just stayed in it, confident that sooner or later the odds would fall in their favor.

Yes, the golf ball story is a great one. Except it may not be factual. The Spalding Company website, which has an extensive section called Heritage, doesn't mention 1909 at all. And it certainly seems that such an event, a modification that changed the whole game, would merit some mention if it actually happened.

That doesn't mean, of course, that it isn't true. There is a big difference between factual and true. Facts are verifiable. Scientifically provable. Authenticated, corroborated, substantiated by independent sources. Facts are universally recognized.

Truth, on the other hand, may not be provable. Truth is something that comes from the heart and no EKG in the world can produce a printout of love or loyalty or patriotism, all of which are very real. A particular truth may very well exist for only one person. And, interestingly enough, it is usually truth, not facts, upon which people are willing to risk their lives.

Just a few thoughts to say that I believe the golf ball story. Maybe it wasn't Mr. Spalding who had the lightbulb moment. Maybe it was a golfing physicist who stood at the tee one day, twirled the ball in his hand, and thought, "This would probably go farther if it had a lot of little dents all over it." Maybe the guy who wrote the article I read made it up entirely. It doesn't matter.

What matters is that the story struck a familiar chord, gave me a visual image to consider the next time I'm feeling a little exploited or misused or the next time I need to encourage someone who is feeling that way himself. What matters is that, call it fact or call it truth, none of us gets through life without a knock or two and it helps to believe that we can be left with something more than just a bruise.

MARCH 4, 2007

Gray-brown like South Georgia dirt, the hickory nut rolls around in the palm of my hand. It is cracked, but still whole. The little point at the end, what the botanists call a stigma, is worn down to a smooth nub.

I picked it up eight or nine years ago one sunny fall afternoon from under a tall tree frosted with Spanish moss. The tree grew on the edge of a lake, on a lot my friends were considering buying. The three of us walked around, our feet shuffling through the leaves that had already begun to fall, and talked about where a house might sit, what the view would be, what good times could be had there.

The nut and a couple others like it ended up in a bowl in my living room along with a handful of acorns the size of quarters that I'd picked up along a hiking trail in North Carolina, some shells from the beach on St. Simons, an abandoned wasp nest, some bird feathers and a pinecone the size of a dime. It has been there ever since.

My friends did buy the lot at the lake and they built a vacation house there. There were pansies in the window boxes and an aluminum windmill that spun like a top on windy days. From the rocking chairs on the screened porch you could hear the water lap against the seawall, an echo of the wakes of the motorboats out in the channel. On clear nights the moon spread out over the water like a million mirrors.

Once, when I was lost and needed a place to try to figure out my coordinates, I went to the lake house to breathe. I had hoped to sit on the dock and watch the winter sun rise and set and find in that rhythm one of my own. Instead, I sat inside and watched it rain for three days, kept company by pencil, paper, and homemade pimento cheese that my friend had laid in store for me.

The endless torrent of water was matched by the one that fell from my eyes. I huddled under the bedcovers and asked myself how I would ever find my way. I read. I wrote. I prayed. I listened as the beat of the rain on the roof became the pulsing of my heart.

And somewhere in the coldness and darkness and wetness of the night I began to understand that I am lost only if I insist on knowing where I am going.

On my last morning there, as the sun began clawing its way through the clouds, I wrote in my journal a quote from Barbara Brown Taylor: "We [must] simply give up the illusion that we are in control of our lives and step out. Which is why, perhaps, it is called a leap of faith."

A couple of years ago, a spark ignited a flame which became a conflagration which ate up the lake house. It was too strong, too fast. By the time the fire truck arrived, it was out of control. In a few short hours, all that was left was the concrete piers, a postmodern Stonehenge. When I got the call I felt as though someone had desecrated my church.

My friends are resilient souls. They decided to rebuild and, this time, to make the lake house their year-round home. It would be bigger, big enough to accommodate lots of family at once. As a result, the hickory tree, already damaged from the intense heat of the fire, had to come down.

The construction is done now. Time to check the view from new windows. Time to move in and consecrate the new rooms with love and laughter. Time to put aside the old memories long enough to make new ones. Time for a housewarming present.

And I know just the thing.

The hickory nut rolls around in the palm of my hand. And today it is going home. A reminder of the connection between the past and the present, a link between what was and what is. And a gentle reminder that what will be is totally dependent on that leap.

MARCH 18, 2007

It was supposed to have been a very busy Sunday—to Savannah for my namesake's confirmation, then to Macon for the funeral of one of my Wesleyan professors, then to Perry to celebrate Katherine's birthday. It turned out not to be.

One of my five-year-old original equipment tires blew out in the left-hand lane of I-16 just outside Savannah and, after the fortuitous appearance of a very kind gentleman who was most adept at the use of a jack and crowbar, I limped back home, wise enough to know that I didn't need to be driving a couple of hundred miles on a doughnut tire.

Gifted, then, with a gloriously sunny Sunday and no expectations, mine or anyone else's, I herded up the dogs and set out on a purposeful amble.

It took a few minutes to slow my normal pace, to let my footsteps fall into a sauntering, unhurried tempo, but once I was there I found myself feeling suspiciously like a ten-year-old and it didn't take long before I was seduced into climbing the grain bin for a quick aerial surveillance of my kingdom. Having determined that all was as it should be, I climbed down, much to the relief of Lily and Tamar who had been unsure as to exactly what was expected of them during my detour, and crossed the road into the woods.

As I walked deeper in, the woods grew quieter and the sunshine dappled. I followed the firebreak for a while, down a slope, up a rise, stepping carefully into the soft patches of wiregrass, not unaware of why the Rattlesnake Roundup is held in March.

Turning and heading back to the road I came across a fallen pine tree. I stepped up on the log and began walking its length, arms out to keep my balance. The rotting wood gave slightly with each step; it felt a little like walking on a trampoline. Halfway down my impromptu balance beam the wood had disintegrated entirely and fallen in mounds of sawdust on either side of the trunk. What remained to connect the two ends was a thin shaft of heartwood, what we country folks call fat lighter.

Heartwood is the inner portion of a tree that, as the tree increases in age and diameter, ceases to function. In old-growth pine trees, the heart becomes saturated with resin and, as a result, will not rot.

Botanists will tell you that heartwood gets its name simply by virtue of its position at the center of the tree, not because of any vital importance. They will also tell you that a tree can continue to live even if its heart is decayed.

Bent over, hands on my knees, staring at the tree's deep yellow entrails glistening in the sun, I couldn't help thinking about the human application: the fact that the hearts of some people are not of vital importance, the fact that they continue to live day after day long after their hearts have died, the fact that— like fat lighter—they are heavy and flammable.

I straightened my back, put my hands on my hips and stretched my neck up to look at the clear blue sky. Who am I fooling? I asked myself. I am one of those people. Not all the time, but sometimes. Not every day, but some days.

Some days I wake up encumbered by unfulfilled dreams and unrealistic expectations and I feel myself hardening, my chest soaking up the resin of resentment and bitterness, before I even put my feet on the floor. By the time I've brushed my teeth I've become intensely flammable, tinder for whatever fire is set around me. And by the end of the day I'm nothing but ashes. Fat lighter won't rot, but it will burn.

I looked around to find that the dogs had abandoned their efforts to find something to chase and made their way back through the brush to see what had fascinated me into stillness.

"See that right there, girls?" I wanted to say. "That is not the kind of heart I want. I want a heart that is alive. A heart that can be touched by what happens to it. A heart that is tender and light so that, when I give it to somebody else, it won't be too heavy to carry. That's what I want."

But I didn't say it because something told me that they already knew.

APRIL 1, 2007

My friend's mother died. I drove south to sit on the back row of the chapel and listen to the minister read from Ecclesiastes. Later, my friend and I stood on a bluff overlooking the Crooked River and breathed in the smell of the marsh, a scent that, though sprouting from death and decay, awakens my senses. We took deep breaths, listened to the water birds, and squinted our eyes against the sun's reflection on the water. A skinny snake paused on his dash from one bank of azalea bushes to another to make sure that we didn't step on him. The breeze off the river caught in the ringlets of my hair and those of the Spanish moss dangling from the branches of the gnarled oak trees, tossing them both like confetti. And the unmistakable grief on my friend's face was joined by an expression of contentment.

On my way home, because I feel something quite like a magnetic pull when I am that close, I stopped on St. Simons for a walk on the beach. Just above the horizon—the imaginary line that reminds me that the only thing that ends is my sight of the ocean, not the ocean itself—in a sky that was the palest shade of blue, the moon had risen, a whitewashed half-disc. Behind me the sun was still up, egg-yolk yellow and warm.

Caught between the two, the fulcrum upon which the day was pivoting into night, I stood still and listened. The rush of the rising tide and the clanging of the masts of the boats in the boatyard and the cries of the children in the surf mingled to become the voice of the minister as he intoned the familiar words: "A time to give birth and a time to die. ... A time to weep and a time to laugh. ... A time to mourn and a time to dance. ... A time to search and a time to give up as lost."

For all the times I had heard the words read, read the words myself, quoted them from memory, I had never noticed the choice of conjunctions. The writer, who calls himself the Preacher, used the inclusive connector, not the limiting. And, not or. In a subtle choice of words, he reminds the reader that the time for being born is not separate and apart from the time for dying. The time for waging war and creating peace are one and the same. Laughing and crying are the same thing. They are joined, irrevocably linked. They happen not at different times, but simultaneously.

It doesn't make sense, of course, to our linear-thinking minds. We move in increments, in steps, through stages. We compartmentalize everything, even the ephemeral. We decide how much we are willing to experience at any given moment and ignore anything not on the agenda. We split our lives into childhood and adulthood. We divide our days into workdays, sick days, vacation days. And, most tellingly, we make strict distinctions between the sacred and profane.

What if, I wondered, I could believe that being silent is, in fact, speaking in the profoundest of voices? Or that in order to know deep love I must also experience intense hatred? Or that the truest way of holding something—or someone—close is by letting it go? Could I learn to live with the contradiction?

It is spring and, for Christians, it is also the season of Lent, forty days of contradiction: A king who refuses to reign, friends who betray and deny, death that results in life. Forty days of paradox. Forty days of pondering the Preacher's sermon, recognizing it as prophecy and watching the prophecy be fulfilled. Of growing to hold in one embrace life and death. War and peace. Love and hate. Never either/or. Always and.

To every thing there is a season. And a time to every purpose under the heaven. With the season comes the purpose. And, if we are open, the grace to live it full.

APRIL 15, 2007

I had an opal necklace. It was a gift—a small stone set in gold on a narrow gold chain. I wore it every day. I would unconsciously finger it while I was on the phone or watching television. When I looked in the mirror it reminded me of lots of things, including the fact that opals are supposed to be good luck for those born in October, but bad luck for anyone else. I was, fortunately, born in October.

One morning I stopped for gas on the way to work and when I got to the office realized that my necklace was gone. I'd had it when I left home and it wasn't in the car. It had to have fallen off at the gas station. I went back—anxious, almost panic-stricken—to scour the parking lot.

I found the chain, but the opal was gone.

Sadness wrapped itself around me like a blanket on a hot day. I wanted to push it away, kick it off. The necklace was, after all, only a thing. The opal was not expensive, what jewelers call a semiprecious stone. It could be replaced.

Except that it couldn't. I wanted that opal, the one that came on the chain, the one that came in the green box that I had opened so excitedly. I wanted the opal that had absorbed my touch for years, that had moved up and down with my breath, that had vibrated with my laughter, rattled with my tears.

A friend at work had a metal detector and he volunteered to go to the gas station and run it over the parking lot, between the pumps, around the trash cans. He didn't find my opal, but he came back with a theory: The clasp on the chain had loosened, the opal had slid off and, when the next car pulled up, had gotten stuck in the tire tread and rolled away.

As theories go, it wasn't all that plausible, but it did give me a visual image to consider—my opal stuck in the tire of a shiny new minivan taking a family to Disney World. Or maybe it had been picked up by a red convertible full of sorority girls on their way to the beach or a diesel belching 4x4 pickup truck hauling seed corn. Imagining my opal on various road trip adventures was helpful for, oh, about fifteen seconds. And then the sadness returned.

The realization that there was absolutely nothing I could do to effectuate the return of my opal was, while not intellectually challenging, emotionally impossible. Things shouldn't get lost. I shouldn't lose things. Things should know better.

It took a few weeks, but eventually the spot at the bottom of my throat where the opal used to nest began feeling less naked. I stopped reaching up to tug it across the chain like an acrobat on a zip-line. I didn't startle myself anymore when I looked in the mirror and didn't see it.

Then one day I didn't think about it at all. And that day became a month and a year and several years. And the lesson is supposed to be that things are just things and a person can always get over losing a thing.

Except that that is not true. Because just this week, for some totally inexplicable reason, I thought about my opal necklace. And I remembered its milky whiteness and the threads of pale aqua that wound through it like a creek. I remembered the iridescence that made it, like a soap bubble, reflect pink, then gold depending on the angle with which the sunlight hit it. And I remembered how secure I'd felt every single time I reached up to touch it, how it symbolized for me something that had nothing to do with being lucky or nicely accessorized.

And I figured out that the lesson was really this: Things are never just things and a person never gets over losing something that was more than just a thing.

There's a place at the bottom of my throat, that little v-shaped place where my collarbone dips down, and it is empty. Always will be. Because that which belongs there is lost.

APRIL 29, 2007

The sky was a blue glass bottle pouring out the white light of the sun. It puddled in the grass of what was once the Wesleyan Botanical Garden and what has been for probably seventy-five years Washington Park. It was a perfect spring Saturday in Macon, like so many perfect spring Saturdays I'd spent there, anesthetized by youth and privilege and oblivious to the gifts of freedom and promise.

A group of about a dozen high school students had gathered for the taking of prom photos. The girls were dressed in bright orange and deep turquoise, jonquil yellow and cobalt blue, their skirts all full and showy like peonies, fluttering in the breeze around their ankles. Their arms and shoulders glowed with the faux bronze of tanning beds. Their hair, pulled up off their necks, couldn't withstand the teasing breeze and came loose in soft tendrils around their carefully lined and shadowed and mascara'ed eyes.

The boys stood awkwardly, hands in the pockets of their rented tuxedos, saying little, following the instructions of the mothers dressed in blue jeans and loose cotton blouses and wondering how exactly they had ended up here, in front of God and everybody, wearing pastel cummerbunds and pin-tucked shirts.

I sat on the grass next to a narrow creek that flowed with just enough water to shimmer like a million tiny mirrors or—better simile—the sequins on the red dress of the tall girl with dark hair and I listened to the giggles, watched from a safe distance the eye rolling and head tossing. I couldn't help being mesmerized by the drawing-room drama played out as the group moved from the bridge to the stone steps to the iron benches, posing and preening, smiling and leaning into each other with the right combination of timidity and sophistication.

Then I looked at my cell phone to check the time and realized I'd missed a call. Probably not anything important. No one was expecting me anywhere. No one should be needing me for anything on my out-of-town Saturday.

I was wrong. The call was from law enforcement, my job, the work that I didn't want to follow me to Macon, and I knew before I dialed the number that something horrible had happened.

My friend Tom, who was born to serve and protect, outlined the facts. One child was dead; another child was arrested. The former now a victim, the latter now what the law calls a juvenile offender. And because he was a juvenile, the people back home had questions for me because I am what the law calls a juvenile prosecutor.

I listened to the story, as much as anyone knew at that point, and felt the light dim, the warmth cool, the musical sound of laughing teenagers transformed into dissonant cackling.

I closed my eyes and accessed that part of my brain that speaks the vocabulary of criminal procedure. I answered questions, asked a few of my own. And then I hung up.

There are moments when one can't help being aware of how big the world is and how isolated we all are from the rest of the people living in it. Most of the time that happens, for me at least, when I'm stuck in Atlanta traffic, experiencing sensory overload and absently wondering where all the people in the cars are going, where they live, how much trash they produce each day and where that goes.

And then there are moments when the world contracts into one small square of earth. Moments when the connectedness of every human being to every other human being is as palpable as spring sunshine on bare arms. Moments when every face is the face of someone you love, every hurt a bruise on your heart, every loss your own sacrifice.

Sitting on the grass in Washington Park last Saturday, it was that kind of moment.

There is no way to make sense of what happened. Here or at Virginia Tech or, eight years ago, at Columbine. But there has to be a way to redeem those moments. A way to translate the language of loss into something speakable.

There has to be.

There just has to be.

MAY 13, 2007

It is dry. Very dry. So dry that the new leaves on the holly trees at Sandhill have rolled into tight brown spirals that make them look like miniature cigars. They disintegrate into fine powder when pressed between my thumb and index finger.

I'm pretty sure that the dryness has something to do with the fact that I've not seen any hummingbirds this spring. Not one. And that disappoints me.

Mixing up the nectar that looks like cherry Kool-Aid, funneling it carefully into the feeders, and then watching the aerial stunt shows of the bird kingdom's imps has become one of the truest delights of springtime for me.

We started this cooperative effort, the hummingbirds and I, about four years ago. I'd never noticed any of them around Sandhill proper though there always seemed to be a few floating around Mama and Daddy's house. One day a visitor noticed a single bird hovering outside the living room window—mesmerized, apparently, by his own reflection—and videotaped the performance to show me when I returned from work.

I was so infatuated that I insisted we drive back to town immediately to buy a feeder. I put it up outside the dining room window and within a couple of days I was being entertained by the hummingbird and his friends while I ate dinner.

Last summer, when I added the deck to Sandhill, I also added another feeder, hanging it on a shepherd's crook at the corner of the deck. This year I got a third—a globe the size of a small canteloupe made of thick glass like a Coca-Cola bottle the color of the ocean at mid-morning—and hung it in the chinaberry tree in the back yard.

On the first warm Saturday I mixed up some nectar and filled all three, ready for the arrival of my hyperactive friends.

Funny thing: Here we are, the middle of May, and I've not seen a single hummingbird.

I come outside to check; the feeders are empty. I fill them up. A few days later, they are empty again. I fill them again. And again. And still no hummingbirds. I can't make them come. All I can do is hope.

Standing under the chinaberry tree the other evening, at just twilight, ocean-blue orb balanced in the palm of one hand, ruby-colored liquid pouring out of a pitcher held in the other hand, I had an epiphany.

"Feeding invisible hummingbirds requires not hope, but faith," I heard my heart whisper.

I stopped to consider that. Hope is very still. Quietly it gazes with rapt attention at the future that is not yet, but might be. Faith, on the other hand, is anything but still. It taps its foot, strums its fingers. It remembers, no, not just remembers, but depends on the past.

Hope pulls. Faith pushes.

Hope desires, longs for, imagines hummingbirds. Faith fills the feeders.

It is hard sometimes to know which of the two virtues is needed. Hard to know whether to turn one's back on what has been and put all one's eggs in the basket of what might be or to leave one's eggs in the nest, knowing that they, kept warm by the body of the mother hen, will hatch in their own time.

And, then, like most epiphanies, this one shifted a little. "Of course," my heart said, still whispering, but a little louder, "sometimes you need both. Sometimes," she said, "faith and hope work together. Sometimes you need to act on what the past taught you in order to imagine what the future might be."

I put the rubber plug back into the feeder, hung it back up on the tree and walked into the house, fairly certain that all that whispering had to do with something other than hummingbirds. And absolutely certain that one day, one day soon, I was going to see a hummingbird.

MAY 27, 2007

Mama was driving the Mule and Daddy was hanging off the edge of the passenger-side seat, a rather precarious way of riding necessitated by the fact that Lily and Tamar were in their usual places—Lily sprawled in the floorboard and Tamar sitting front and center beside Mama. They drove up into my yard and Mama asked, "You had supper? Your daddy just caught a nice mess of fish. There's enough for you, too."

Accepting the invitation, I set out for a long walk with the intention of ending up back at Mama and Daddy's house just as the fish were coming out of the frying pan. As is usually the case, I got there a little early and, entranced with the book that I taken with me on my walk, I decided to sit out on the porch and try to finish a chapter rather than join Daddy in watching Fox News.

It was balmy and just a little overcast. It was that moment in the evening when the sun has gone down, but the bugs have not yet descended in vengeance upon every available inch of uncovered human flesh. The late afternoon traffic on what used to be practically our own private road had slowed to about one car or truck every twenty minutes or so. The dogs were dozing on the deck underneath the rustling limbs of the pecan tree.

My reading was suddenly disturbed by Tamar running across the yard to stand at attention in the middle of the road. I didn't hear a vehicle of any kind approaching so I dropped my head back to my book. She was probably scoping out a squirrel.

Then I heard her growl. That defensive growl that starts in the back of her throat and expands slowly until it gets to her mouth and forces it open to show teeth. I closed my book to look. This time she was shivering, her golden fur shaking like a cheerleader's pom-pom. What in the world had her so wound up?

I followed the turn of her nose and raised my head toward the sky and that's when I saw them: a bundle of balloons—five or six of them, red and blue and yellow, tied together with string and floating down the road toward us.

When you live in the country you pay attention to the sky. You watch for sunrise and sunset. You keep an eye on what might be rain clouds. You notice a hawk dive-bombing what looks like an empty field only to see him swoop back up with an unlucky mouse in his talons. You know what belongs there—rainbows and turkey vultures and crop dusters, butterflies and dragonflies and diesel smoke.

So when something as out-of-place as a bunch of balloons unattached to a hand comes floating across the landscape, you—if you are a dog—growl, then bark loudly enough to make sure your dog friend comes running and the two of you go chasing the balloons as the wind bounces them down the road just high enough above your heads that there is no chance you'll ever catch · them.

If you are a person, especially if you are a person who reads a lot and sees everything in literary terms, you stop what you are doing and watch the parade of balloons and dogs make its way down the road. You wonder who set the balloons free and how they came to be at this exact spot at this exact moment and, most importantly, you wonder what it means. You glance down at the title of the book you are reading, which just happens to be *Where God Was Born*.

The author, who knows quite a bit about such things, maintains the almost-universally accepted idea that God or, more accurately, religion was born in that part of the world formerly known as Mesopotamia. He's been there and he's seen the ruins of Ur and Babylon and what's left of Old Jerusalem. He's hiked through the Negev and climbed the Mount of Olives, even visited the spot that tradition says was the location of the Garden of Eden. He has a lot of support for his idea.

And on any other day I would probably agree with him. But this day, this night I'm standing in the lavender light of a place where there is always more than enough fish for supper, where looking at the sky will teach you everything you need to know, where balloons appear out of nowhere, and for this moment, at least, I think God may very well have been born right here.

JUNE 10, 2007

A summer morning at Sandhill sounds like the first day of kindergarten—fifteen or twenty high-pitched voices all talking at the same time. The kindergartners in this case being the birds—cardinals and sparrows and crows—that share my living space. An experienced birder could surely distinguish among the songs and calls; I am satisfied to sit in the concert hall and listen. This morning I get more than a performance.

I've gone out to sit on the deck, notebook and pencil in hand, intending to take a few notes on an interesting conversation I've been having with myself in the shower. The sun is well over the trees, its edges smudged by a giant thumb, and there is just the slightest hint of dew clinging to the pansies and geraniums.

The pencil is flying across the page trying to keep up with my thoughts in handwriting I'd be embarrassed to have seen by Mrs. Blitch, who taught me cursive in third grade. I hear something that sounds at first like clothes on a clothesline flapping in the breeze. Distracted for a moment from my writing, I turn to see a bird perched on the top of the back steps, a tiny disheveled bundle of twigs in her mouth.

It is a small bird. Plump and brown with white eyebrows. A Carolina wren. (I learn this only after the fact when I look it up in the Audubon guide.) She hops down the steps, pausing on each one to look side to side. When she gets to the bottom she makes one good flap of her wings and dives for the dryer vent. Hindered by something I can't see, she bounces out of the plastic hood and shoots into the wheel well on the car. A second later she appears again, flying out into the open sky, beak firmly clamped on the twigs.

I go back to my writing and, not one sentence later, am interrupted again by the flapping. She lands, hops, pauses, dives, bounces and shoots all over again. And again. She performs this ballet at least five or six times.

She is, of course, looking for a place to build a nest. The dark cavities of the dryer vent and the wheel well were appealing options at first, but clearly not suitable upon further inspection. So why does she keep coming back? She has everything she needs to make a home, a sanctuary, a place to settle. All she needs is a place to land, a place where her tiny twigs can be safely released from her grip.

There are all kinds of trees and shrubs available within fifteen or twenty yards. There are eaves and posts and ledges. There are nooks and crannies, natural and man-made, all around her just waiting to be claimed and all she wants to do is to force herself into a spot that, clearly, isn't right.

It is time to go to work. I leave my neurotic little friend to her dilemma—to live out her days fighting for something she can't have or to relax, let go, and open her eyes to the multitude of choices available to her.

I leave her, but I can't forget her. So tiny, so determined, so confused. So like us. So like me, clinging tightly to my twigs and beating my wings against brick walls. Hopping, diving, and bouncing in the same spots repetitively. Frustrating myself with my inability to make the right choice, find the right answer.

Later, at my desk, thoughts of the stubborn little wren bring an image to mind. I am five or six. I am uncomfortable—my crinoline is scratching the backs of my legs, the bow tied at my waist is pressing into my back, my ponytail holder is so tight that the skin at my temples is stinging. I am watching my Sunday School teacher put up a flannelgraph picture of Jesus preaching the Sermon on the Mount. He is sitting on a big rock with his hand raised in blessing over the crowd that surrounds him. "Think about the birds," he is saying. "I take care of them. Don't you think I will take care of you?"

Think about the bird. Think about the tiny little wren with her treasure of twigs that, in the right crook of the right branch of the right tree, will make a nest. A place to rest. And not just for the bird, but for me.

JUNE 24, 2007

And then it rained. Thick and heavy, the water hit the roof, hit the ground like a percussion instrument and the music surrounded the house, surrounded me.

After so many weeks of choking dust and bleaching light and burning heat, the landscape was thin and flat, but in a matter of only moments, it seemed, depth and color returned. Shallow puddles appeared in the yard. The dull monotone green of grass and trees and kudzu changed into luminous Crayola hues of kelly and chartreuse and olive.

As soon as it stopped I put on a pair of mud-worthy tennis shoes and set out. Down the field road, over the newly-cleared pond dam, and around the edges of the laid-out corner field, I walked deliberately, measuring my steps, taking in the inimitable scent of corn-after-rain. My breaths slowed, my steps slowed, my thoughts slowed.

Mist settled on my arms and in my hair. Wet itchy vines wrapped around my ankles. Branches shook in the breeze and baptized me with a million tiny drops. Like the ground beneath me, I was soaking it in.

You see, drought isn't only a condition of geography and weather. It is—at least metaphorically speaking—an emotion and, like a literal drought, can result in wildfires—wildfires of self-condemnation or, in the other extreme, self-importance.

Go long enough without rain and your heart will lapse into survival mode, holding on to everything, giving up nothing out of fear of losing all. Go long enough without water—without the thirst-slaking taste of it in your mouth, without the cleansing feel of it on your skin—and your heart will shrivel up and die.

I was almost there and the rain had come just in time.

Now, no longer panting, I could begin listening to the conversation that had been going on between my heart and my head for days, maybe months. A conversation I had effectively ignored by focusing on the drought.

You have to listen hard when a conversation is being carried on in a whisper. You have to pay close attention to grasp the gist of the exchange. No longer consumed with thirst, I could.

I listened all the way back to the house and I was still listening when I talked to a friend of mine yesterday. She mentioned someone we both know who was going through a drought. The life she'd been handed wasn't turning out in accordance with the architectural renderings she had so carefully drawn and, as a result, she had done some uncharacteristic things.

She needs some water. She needs a tall glass, a hot shower, a long swim, a good cry. I know.

What I want to tell her is that in the middle of a drought— when all you can see are the stalks twisting tighter and the riverbanks growing taller and the dust clouds rising higher and it's hard, impossible even, to remember the taste of sweet corn, the smell of bream beds, the tickle of an afternoon breeze, when the sky is empty and the heat of the day lingers long into the night, it is not a good idea to move around a lot. In the middle of a drought, you stay inside when you can and move slowly when you can't. You save the striving and purposefulness for another day. You turn the pillow over to the cool side, lie very still, and wait.

Wait for the rain.

That is what I want to tell her. I hope she's listening.

JULY 8, 2007

Sometime around the first of the year, I found out about a book titled *The Intellectual Devotional*. The title alone was reason enough to buy it.

The introduction describes the volume as "one year's worth of daily readings that will refresh your spirit, stimulate your mind, and help complete your education." Who wouldn't want that? I've learned a lot of interesting things in the past six months. For example, one Thursday (science day) I learned about nociception, which is the perception of pain. The anterior cingulate cortex is the part of the brain responsible for that and, interestingly enough, it does not distinguish between physical and emotional pain. As the authors put it, "It responds equally to a broken arm and to a broken heart." Imagine.

I tend to see things metaphorically so one Friday (music day) as I read about harmony, I couldn't help reading an important life lesson into the comment that "[w]ithout the instability of temporary dissonance, tonal music would be boring; without the stability of consonance, it would be unsatisfying." In the back of my mind I kept hearing a wise teacher telling me that without the hard times, the good times couldn't be appreciated and without the good times the hard times couldn't be borne.

You can see, then, why I'm always eager for each morning's dip and why there are underlinings and scribbled notes all over the pages. Each day there is something that makes me think and, in a world where there is less and less of that going on, I'm grateful for the challenge.

Which brings me to today's reading. I'm writing this on Thursday, which (as noted above) is science day, and the topic is reproduction. The reading begins, "In the plant and animal kingdom, there are two main ways to reproduce: asexually and sexually." Yeah, yeah, tenth grade biology stuff. Not going to be all that enlightening.

Or so I thought.

Second paragraph: "Budding is a common form of asexual reproduction found in strawberries, aspen trees, and coral. In budding, the offspring grows from a part of the parent. Sometimes they break apart, but other times they remain connected for life" and, as a result, have "a more difficult time evolving to changes in the environment."

As I read it, I could hear my brain adding the phrase, "like some people I know."

What? From where did that idea spring forth?

My Adam graduated college in May. Light of my life from the day he was born, fearless and opinionated, great joy and irritant simultaneously, he is now out there. He has a job and a life and he doesn't call me three times a day anymore for phone numbers or favors or advice.

We still call him, occasionally, by one of his childhood nicknames—Bud—but the truth is that Adam is not a bud. He is a separate, unique organism. He carries a little of each of us, but the combination is his alone. And that combination, I have to believe, will be enough to get him through the inevitable "changes in the environment"—the stresses, the losses, the frustrations.

Believing that does not, of course, eliminate the instinctual desire to shield him from those things (a desire that has a lot to do with nociception and the anterior cingulate cortex perception of broken arms and broken hearts). The truth is that I'd just as soon save the people I love from affliction of any kind.

But I would be wrong to do that. Wrong to deprive anyone who means anything to me of the flaming-hot, ice-cold, blood-boiling, bone-chilling experience of real pain. It comes to us all and, without it, we would never know how strong we are.

It's a lesson I learned not from *The Intellectual Devotional* but from living, not from a book but from birthdays. And that single lesson—that each of us can be strong enough to handle whatever comes her way—may very well be the sum total of all the other lessons combined.

JULY 29, 2007

Up until about a year ago, when people mentioned the Food
Network or Fox News, I could only nod in vague understanding
because, up until about a year ago, my television viewing, which
could be called minimal at best, was limited to one really clear
channel, two sporadically clear channels and two more on-a-
cloudless-night-after-nine-o'clock-maybe channels. I was restrict-
ed to viewing what is known as network television by a tall tower
of aluminum stuck into the ground just outside the dining room
window and connected to the television by a long spool of coaxial
cable that my poor daddy, on his back and in the dark, had had to
snake through the crawl space under the house.

Things changed when, as a part of the renovations on
Sandhill, the antenna was unbolted from its brace at the roofline
so that the new siding could be put up. That very afternoon a stiff
spring wind came up and knocked the antenna to the ground and
that night, after a long day of being beaten up by the system I am
sworn to support and defend, when all I wanted to do was stretch
out on the couch and be mindlessly entertained, my five channels
had been reduced to one.

And on that one channel that night was the season premiere of
American Idol. I'd never seen it, but after the first hour of what
was a two-hour show I was convinced that American culture was
in quite a bit more danger than I had previously known.

All that to say that when my boss forwarded to me an e-mail
containing a video clip from YouTube (another cultural phenom-
enon to which I have only recently been introduced) regarding the
British equivalent of (and predecessor to) American Idol, I was
prepared to be amazed all over again at just how far people will
go to get attention.

I was amazed. But not in the way I had anticipated. I was
amazed in the way that causes the hairs to stand up on your arms,

the way that brings tears to your eyes, the way that reminds you that there is a seed of nobility in every human heart.

The clip was of a man named Paul Potts. He showed up at his audition and told the judges he would be singing opera. There were patronizing smiles and a slight raising of the eyebrows. And then he began to sing.

In a voice so clear and so true and so honest that it made absolutely no difference that he sang in a language most of the audience could not understand, the thirty-six-year-old car phone salesman from Wales brought down the house.

Subsequent clips showed him moving through the competition, each night filling the auditorium with passion and humility and each night rousing the listeners to their feet to applaud as they tried to wipe their eyes. In an interview, Potts said, "My voice has always been my best friend. If I was having problems with bullies at school I always had my voice to fall back on." Confessing that self-confidence had always been "a difficult thing" for him, Potts said, "When I'm singing I don't have that problem. I'm in the place where I should be."

Ah, yes, Paul Potts understands. He knows that we all need someplace within ourselves that we can go to get away from the bullies.

The story has a happy ending: Paul Potts wins the competition, signs a record contract with Sony, and sings for the queen. Not bad for a man who first sang opera at the age of twenty-eight for a karaoke contest.

I've watched that YouTube clip about four times now. And I'll watch it again. I'll watch it every time I need to be awakened from the lethargy of mediocrity, every time I need to be jolted into the action of soulful living, every time I need to be reminded of the power of dreams.

AUGUST 5, 2007

This spring, in a fit of the spontaneity to which I always aspire, but rarely attain, I bought two big pots of Gerbera daisies for the front porch at Sandhill. For as many years as I can remember, it has been geraniums that stood sentinel on either side of the front steps, sunset coral or patriotic red, but in the five seconds or so that it took to walk from the parking lot and through the cyclone-fenced garden center at Lowe's, the daisies caught my eye and kept it.

They are bright magenta, the color of a lightning flash over the ocean, the color of cooked rhubarb or just-cut pomegranate. The flower heads balance themselves on the tops of long, straight stems and the petals reach out and down in gentle curves that make them look as though they are arching their backs as they stretch into the sunlight. The leaves are broad and thick and the color of pine needles in deep summer and their edges are ruffled like the hem of a chiffon cocktail dress. They are showy without being ostentatious, more flirts than trollops.

Just the other morning I walked out on the porch to check the pulse of yet another hot and humid South Georgia day and noticed that one of the pots had five blooms. The other had none. I poked around in the barren pot and noticed a couple of short stems with closed buds beneath the dark green leaves, but it was clear that it would be days before they grew into the sunlight. On the other side of the steps, the sorority of five bounced and swayed in time to the breezy music of the wind chimes, oblivious to the deficiencies of their neighbor.

When we were in law school, my friend Linda often bemoaned our lack of a social life. She had been an Alpha Gamma Delta at Mercer, a member of a tight pack of cute and funny and popular girls whose weekends were always full. On one particularly dull night, Linda looked at me and said, "You know, Kathy A. Bradley, I think that maybe a person is assigned just a certain number of dates in her life and I used up all mine in college."

Considering my own less-than-sparkling social calendar during that four-year period, I replied, "Well, if that's true I guess I have a lot to look forward to."

Without a second's hesitation Linda looked at me sympathetically and said, "Oh, no. You don't understand. Not everybody gets the same number."

Ah, yes, that old "life isn't fair" thing.

I thought about that as I looked at my daisies. Same species, same front porch. Same sunshine, same water. One fertile and engaging. One just ... well ... sort of plain. The luck of the draw. The roll of the dice.

My last year of college (during which my friend Linda was across town using up her date allotment) I took a course in which the professor utilized contract grading. On the first day of class he gave us, along with the syllabus, a list of what it would take to earn an A, a B, a C. There would be no curves, no ranking. If every person in the class met the contract requirements for an A, then every person would get an A. If no one did, then no one got an A. What a great idea! Certain. Absolute. Foolproof.

How many of us, in the midst of great upheaval of one sort or another, have craved exactly that? A contract, a list of requirements that can be checked off when complete, a promise that if we do all the right things we'll get what we want. A guarantee that life will be fair.

And yet, even as the craving gnaws away at our equilibrium, in the midst of the anger and tears we must acknowledge that that kind of fairness would rob life of its beauty and its tenderness. Knowing what will capture my heart tomorrow would surely prevent me from giving it today.

I water the daisies in the evenings, after the heat of the day has waned and the stillness of dusk has settled on Sandhill. I fill up the watering can and watch as the water splashes into the flowerpots, half a can in each one. And this time I can't help noticing that a couple of the flowers in the blessed pot are beginning to droop. The petals are turning a burnished red color and the stems are beginning to bend into a dowager's hump.

In the other pot, the short stems are taller and the buds are plumper. Their day is coming.

And knowing that makes me smile.

AUGUST 19, 2007

It was a spur-of-the-moment jaunt. A whim. An impulse. Katherine and I were visiting our friend Lee Lee in Atlanta one hot summer weekend and, with nothing in particular to do, the three of us decided that a Braves game might be fun. I had never been to a Braves game and, though my awakening to the truth of baseball as metaphor for practically the entire human experience was yet to come, I was eager to get to Fulton County Stadium and immerse myself in the iconic sights and sounds and smells.

I was particularly excited at the prospect, faint though it was, of catching a foul ball. Except for the fact that I do, sadly enough, throw like a girl, I've always been a pretty good ballplayer and back then Katherine and I were rabidly competitive members of the rec department church league, thus I was completely prepared for the possibility of catching that ball by the presence of my glove in the trunk of my car.

After purchasing tickets from a scalper—the criminal nature of which I was completely oblivious at the time—we made our way to seats along the leftfield line, just a few rows behind and past the opposing team dugout. The Braves were playing the Phillies that night and about midway through the game future Hall-of-Famer Mike Schmidt hit a homerun over the left centerfield wall, making it clear that the Braves didn't really stand a chance of winning. At that point I stopped paying close attention to the action on the field.

And so I was to take the first step toward that aforementioned awakening: As the three of us chatted, occasionally glancing toward the diamond, someone (Brave or Phillie I can't remember) hit a ball that flew into the heavy Georgia sky in a high arc away from the players and toward the section in which we were sitting, toward the seat in that section in which I was sitting.

My glove was under my seat. There was no time to pull it out and stuff my hand into its soft leather. There was time only to register the speed and force of the ball and recognize the fact that if I attempted to catch it bare-handed I would most likely end up at the Grady Hospital Emergency Room getting a finger splinted.

So it bounced on the hard concrete and ricocheted into the hands of the man behind us.

Katherine has never let me forget it.

I thought the lesson was that being prepared isn't always enough, that being prepared has to be accompanied by being alert if one is to catch life's unexpected foul balls, receive life's unexpected gifts.

A few weeks ago, my friend Loretta invited me to a Braves game. Someone had shared with her a couple of seats directly behind the Braves' dugout and, generous and understanding soul that she is, she wanted me to have the whole VIP experience, including in-seat service by the concession staff.

It was a beautiful night. The Braves were playing good baseball. Turner Field was green and luminous. The stands were full. Could it get any better?

Tim Hudson was pitching that night. He took the mound in the first inning and gave up a hit to the first Colorado Rockies batter. The second batter flew out. The third batter hit a squibbler to the shortstop Escobar, who deftly tossed it to the second baseman Johnson, who rifled it across the red clay to the newly-acquired first baseman Teixeira. Double play.

The crowd rose to its feet and cheered as the team ran to the dugout. And, suddenly, there it was—the double-play ball—rolling gently across the roof of the dugout toward me. Smooth white leather, tight red stitches, black Major League Baseball emblem. I felt my eyes open wide, heard the gasp that came from my mouth, and reached out to cup it in my hands.

I hadn't even tried.

It was probably twenty-five years between those two games. Sometimes it takes that long to learn something important. Sometimes it takes that long to know how to appreciate unexpected gifts.

SEPTEMBER 2, 2007

By the time Lily and I got started on our walk on Saturday, the sun was already well over halfway up the sky and streaming through whatever is left of the ozone like a wide-angle laser. The wet air settled on my arms and the curls on the nape of my neck the minute I walked out onto the porch. The faint drone of bugs of every sort warned me that I would soon become someone's lunch.

August in South Georgia. It's why the sissies move to Atlanta.

About half a mile from the house, headed up the hill toward the crossroad, we came up on one of our neighbors, his truck and those of his companions loaded with deer stands.

"It's that time of year again," Bruce said in greeting.

"Yeah, and you couldn't pay me money to be sitting in a tree stand in this kind of weather," I told him, understanding, of course, that this is only one of many reasons why I'd never make much of a hunter.

It was then that I noticed the little girl. Seven or eight years old, I'd guess, she'd stepped out of her daddy's truck and was looking at Lily. She reached out her hand, palm up, and Lily moved over to sniff. The little girl stood very still while Lily nuzzled her fingertips.

"You know how to make friends with dogs, don't you?" I asked.

She didn't say anything, just turned her hand over to rub it across Lily's black head, and my usually manic dog sat down in the road, panting quietly, as the little girl's gentleness and innocence came pouring out in the light strokes of her fingers.

For a moment, I was oblivious to the heat, the humidity, the hum of the insects around my face. For a moment, all the irritations and uncertainties and sadnesses that had crept onto my shoulders for the last few days seemed weightless. For a moment, the sun and summer and time stood still and all there was was a little girl and a dog looking into each other's eyes.

I asked and she told me her name was Brin. At least I think that's what she said. She spoke in a soft voice, almost a whisper, and she didn't look up at me for more than a second. It was Lily that interested her.

I said my good-byes to Bruce, waved to Brin's dad in the truck, and started back down the road. Lily reluctantly followed.

Earlier in the morning the radio had reminded me that it had been ten years since the nearly simultaneous deaths of Mother Teresa and Princess Diana. Much had been made at the time, and was being made again on this anniversary, of the vast divide between the lives of two women who, in life and in very different ways, had touched the lives of millions and who, in death and surprising similitude, had taught us all lessons about connectedness.

Princess Diana's gift, a commentator noted, was being able to create a sense of intimacy between herself and whoever else was present—be it a crowd of paparazzi or a single AIDS patient—and it was that ability that endeared her to anyone who ever met her. Mother Teresa did that with the poor and dying with which whom she chose to be surrounded, offering intimacy to those who had never known the healing power of relationship.

Both of them, like all of us, were haunted by the pain and affliction of a less-than-perfect existence and from that pain and affliction had grown to understand the dependency of all creatures on each other. And both of them had learned the lesson that Mother Teresa articulated in these oft-quoted words: "I have found the paradox that if you love until it hurts, there can be no more hurt, only more love."

Something about the encounter with Brin made me think that she had already, somehow, learned that lesson herself and that my own knowledge of that truth would grow, somehow, deeper and truer as a result of that chance meeting.

In the stickiness and sultriness, Lily and I walked almost all the way to the highway. On our way back, we found tire tracks and footprints in the powdery red dust at the top of the hill, the only evidence of our visitation by an angel in blue jeans and a camouflage baseball cap.

SEPTEMBER 16, 2007

My preference for the ocean does not keep me from appreciating other bodies of water, so earlier this summer when my friends Tim and Lori asked if I'd like to visit them at their lake house, my only response was, "When?"

A couple of Saturdays later I was headed north, following directions by which only a girl raised in the country would not be intimidated. The sun was high and white, making the two-lane asphalt roads glimmer like a mirror ball in a disco. The drought had not yet leeched all the color from the grass along the rights-of-way and the tall green blades swayed back and forth in the breeze of the passing cars.

In Wadley I got detoured by road construction and pulled into a church parking lot, interrupting the conversation of two parishioners to ask directions. "Just follow me, honey," one of the ladies said. "I'm going that way."

She got into her car and said, "Now, when I turn right you just keep going straight." And when she turned right, waving wildly out the window, I kept going straight, back on track.

I drove through Sparta and Greensboro, towns where the streets downtown are still busy on a Saturday morning, now paying closer attention to that part of the directions that said things like, "Be on the lookout for a faded wooden sign." Before long the tires on the Escape were crunching over gravel strewn on red clay and I knew I'd arrived.

It is, as I suspected it would be, a beautiful spot. The house looks as though it had been built by the trees themselves, as though they had simply leaned themselves against each other in perfect symmetry and balance and melded into each other to keep out the elements. The land slopes gently down to the water where wide shallow waves made by passing boats lick the spit of sand that Tim and Lori's girls call the beach.

The girls and I played in the water, stuck sycamore leaves in our ponytail holders and called ourselves Indian princesses. We searched for treasures of rocks and twigs and recently-deceased insects. We had hot dogs for lunch and then all went for a ride in the boat, going fast and slow and fast again. We waved at people we knew and people we didn't. And the day wound down in sentences that got softer and slower as the sun slipped closer to the horizon.

We were sitting on the porch, chairs rocking in unintended rhythm when Tim said, "The sunset. You've got to see the sunset from the boat."

Back out on the water, it was then that I identified the mental gnat I'd been swatting all day.

There is another lake house where I've spent a lot of time. Another lake. Another set of friends. That house faces east and it is the sunrise that is so exquisitely beautiful, the morning whose quietness drapes around your shoulders and calls you out to see. A mirror image of this place, these friends, this evening.

We are creatures of habit, we humans. We fall into patterns and then assume that those patterns are the only ones. We get used to the sunrise outside our windows and forget that there are windows that frame the sunset. We forget that what we know is not all there is to know.

Later, in the shallow darkness of early summer, we sat in front of a fire listening to crickets and telling stories. The girls came outside smelling like soap and sunshine and convincing their daddy, with little more than a look, that it was a perfect time to roast marshmallows.

His big hands dwarfing the puffy white squares of sugar and egg whites, Tim stuck one on a metal rod and kneeled down in front of the fire. He turned the marshmallow round and round, just barely above the reach of the flames, the color changing from white to yellow to gold to caramel.

"Didn't you like the sunset?" he asked me without taking his eyes off the marshmallow.

"Yes," I answered him. "Yes, I did."

SEPTEMBER 30, 2007

The Escape is going to be six years old next month. Together we've traveled over 90,000 miles. Last week I took her in for a checkup. I'd called ahead and reserved a rental car so that I wouldn't have to sit in the customer service lounge reading out-of-date magazines and listening to other customers either talk loudly on their cell phones or snore for the several hours I'd been told the checkup would take.

When I got there, however, there had been a mistake in the scheduling and it appeared for a moment that I would, in fact, be consigned to wait. I must have sounded pretty pitiful when I asked, "Do you have anything at all available?" because the older of the two gentlemen at the rental desk looked at the other and said, "Well, we could let her have the little red car."

The first image that came to mind was a loaner Mama got once when her van was in the shop after hitting or having been hit by (depending on one's interpretation of events) a deer. It was a Dodge Colt and sounded like a sewing machine mounted on a wheelbarrow. Beggars, of course, can't be choosers so I just smiled and walked outside to await the arrival of my transportation.

As anyone who has ever read a fairy tale or a John Grisham novel knows, life is full of surprises and I couldn't help laughing out loud when the rental desk man came wheeling around the corner in a candy-apple red Mazda RX-3. (I know the make and model only because I read it on the flashing digital dashboard display as I was trying to figure out how to turn on the radio. Before that moment I would have simply called it a sports car.)

The rental desk man smilingly explained to me that I did not need a key to crank this beautiful piece of machinery—only a very thin computer card which had only to be somewhere inside the vehicle when I turned the knob that looked for all the world like an ordinary ignition switch into which someone on the assembly line had forgotten to cut the keyhole.

Correctly identifying the bewildered expression on my face as that of a person who suspects that she has just been given far too much power, he went on to say, "You're going to be fine." This man had clearly not been present during my first driving lesson some thirty-five years ago when I nearly hit a fire hydrant, burst into tears, and promised Daddy that I would never get behind the wheel of a car again.

Taking a deep breath, I adjusted the seat by pressing three separate levers, turned on the windshield wipers (the only thing in the entire car that looked like and was located in the same place as the corresponding item on the Escape), and eased slowly into traffic. I must say that I felt a bit conspicuous—almost as though I was wearing a skirt that was a little too short—but by the time I got back to the interstate and accelerated down the ramp, that feeling was long gone.

It had been replaced by a feeling I couldn't have identified even if I'd tried, but I wasn't trying. I flashed down that highway, moving from lane to lane with unnaturally languid grace. I settled into a pulsing rhythm that was at the same time comfortable and exhilarating. I watched light glint off the glossy-like-nail-polish paint job and heard myself singing along with the radio so loudly that, had the sun roof been open, the Mack truck in the other lane could have heard me.

And at that moment I understood.

There is something about a car that is fast and flirty and shiny and more engine than anything else that turns a utilitarian object, a means of getting from one place to another, into a symbol and that makes the driver of that object an archetype—man or, in this case, woman searching for freedom.

People drive expensive sports cars for lots of reasons, but I know now that for at least some of them, it has nothing to do with showing off or gaining attention (though I did find that attention can be thusly gained). For those people, it has nothing to do with the response of others, but the response of oneself.

In that little red sports car I did not think about the files on my desk, the numbers in my checkbook, the to-do list on my calendar. For a short while, I was totally, absolutely, decisively unencumbered.

And it was fun.

The Escape and I are still together. As far as I'm concerned, we'll be together for another 90,000 miles. But, to be honest, I'm hoping that the next time we go in for a checkup and I need temporary transportation, I'll be lucky enough to get that little red car. And next time, I'll be ready.

OCTOBER 14, 2007

I noticed it, what at first appeared to be a matted, wadded up piece of spider web, as I started down the back steps. It was hanging from the dryer vent, moving just slightly in the breeze. As I reached to pull it away I realized that it was a fragment of leaf attached to a thin twig attached to a larger twig stuffed inside the vent, not just dangling on the edge.

I cocked my head for a better look and saw that the vent was completely filled with twigs. It was, in fact, a nest and as I gently scooped it out all I could see was the six loads of clothes I'd dried over the last few days and the conflagration that could have been Sandhill had the nest caught fire.

The nest was about the size of a saucer and only about an inch deep at its center. The outer twigs fell away in my hands with a small poof of dust. Nestled in the hollow at the bottom were four tiny eggs. Tiny like a jelly bean. Tiny like a peanut. Tiny like a pearly button on a baby's christening gown.

Having touched the nest and contaminated it with my humanness, I knew—according to all the nature lore I'd learned as a child and which, admittedly, may or may not be true—that the mother bird, wherever she was, would now abandon the babies-in-process. What was probably closer to scientific actuality is that the eggs were old and the embryos inside were long dead.

Months ago, in spring, I had sat on the deck and watched a little bird, a Carolina wren, dart in and out of the dryer vent. From a distance I'd not seen that she'd been carrying bits and pieces of nest to her new place of abode. I'd thought she was just engaging in the avian version of a real estate showing when what she was really doing was moving in. The mortgage had been signed, the electricity turned on, the change-of-address cards mailed.

Too bad she hadn't talked to the neighbors. I could have told her that central heat, in this case, wasn't such a good idea. That the need for incubation aside, too much of a good thing can be deadly. That there is more to safety than isolation and darkness.

Nestled in my cupped hands, what had been a perfect home— if only for a moment—was now nothing more than a bunch of tender twigs gone brittle in the lingering heat of a lingering summer. The chocolate brown of new shoots had faded to the dull gray of lint. The sap that had made them flexible had dried up like a creek bed in drought.

I stood there staring for a few minutes. Eggs. Usually symbols of new life and beginnings, these four round balls of calcium carbonate contradicted all the myths and fairy tales and traditions. Instead, they had become a metaphor for the result of ignorance, haste, inattention. They had gone from being cradles to coffins.

And as is always the case when I stop to consider the world revolving around me and the fact that it doesn't really revolve around me, I realized how like that little Carolina wren we all are. We make choices based on limited information and later find ourselves stunned by the unavoidable results of those choices. We elevate comfort over safety and safety over breadth of experience and breadth of experience over loyalty and never even realize that it's not elevation we're reaching at all—that this life is not a staircase moving us ever higher, but a Ferris wheel looping us up and down in a never-ending circle.

Something of great importance demanded my attention at that moment, so I laid the nest on the floor of the carport and went inside. That was two days ago. Since then I've been leaving home early, getting home late, suffering with the red eyes and runny nose and hacking cough of allergies and, in general, not paying much attention to anything other than myself.

I have no idea if the nest is still there, if the mother is aware of her dispossession, if the eggs have been desecrated by some night-moving animal. I should know. But I don't.

And that, I have to admit, is as much a metaphor as anything else.

OCTOBER 28, 2007

Point worth noting: At first glance, it is impossible to tell whether the tide is coming in or going out.

I came to this realization last weekend watching the ocean lap at my feet as I sat on a barnacle-crusted rock that, among many others, had been hoisted onto the beach in an effort to slow erosion.

I happened to be sitting there in an effort to forestall a different kind of erosion: four friends and I had come to the island to breathe deeply and talk seriously and laugh loudly and now, on Sunday, they had left for home. As soon as the towels finished drying back at the condo I would do the same, but as long as I sat on the rock, staring at the wide flat ocean, nothing could eat away at the peacefulness and serenity that buds in the human heart when it feels safe.

There were few people on the beach. It was, after all, October. A couple of kayakers paddled in unison in water just deep enough for their paddles. An awkward teenager splashed in the shallow puddles that surrounded the rocks and squealed as the waves wet her rolled-up pants legs. A man on a bicycle made a wide turn and headed back the way he had come.

I sat with my knees pulled up to my chest, arms wrapped around them and chin perched atop them, as though I'd been spring-loaded, ready to be flung into the sky and out over the ocean in a long wide arc that ended at the horizon. A seated fetal position, a not-so-subtle manifestation of something gestating but not yet ready to be birthed.

I stared at the sandbar, covered in water, where the rolling sea first makes white foam. I imagined a spot in the middle of the ocean, miles and miles away from land and people, where the water and salt and air that will become the waves seem motionless, the surface almost like glass. But they are not motionless, the water and salt and air. Gravity—the magnetic force that through the rotation of the planet and its moon creates the tide, pulling in, pushing out, in a predictable rhythm—has already begun its work.

Making their imperceptible journey toward land, the waves feel the resistance of the ocean floor as the water becomes shallower. They move faster, developing power with their speed, and they begin to fold over themselves, grabbing the hovering air, ready to throw themselves in graceful, leaping curves at the shore, ready to lick at the sand beneath me, beneath the rock.

That's when I wondered, for the first time since I'd walked down to the beach, whether the tide was coming in or going out. And that's when I realized, for the first time ever, that a quick glance won't tell.

A quick glance is pretty much all we give most things. A quick glance at the newspaper, a quick glance at the mail, a quick glance at the price tag. A quick glance in the rear-view mirror before changing lanes. Sometimes a quick glance is enough.

But not always. A quick glance at a child's tear-streaked face is not enough. A quick glance at a sunset that smears the sky with the colors of a neon sign is not enough. A quick glance at one's own heart is not enough.

These are matters that require prolonged gazing, lengthy contemplation, lingering consideration. These are matters the essence of which are revealed only with the investment of deep and sometimes painful examination.

Like the tide, these are matters of mystery and magic. Like the tide, their rhythms are ebb and flow. But like the tide, they can be trusted.

One of the things about the beach that always amazes me is that the constant movement can seem so still, that the noise can seem so quiet. That in that place and in that moment I can seem so still and quiet.

I looked down at the water slapping the rocks beneath me. The tide, I could tell, was coming in.

NOVEMBER 11, 2007

There are few people outside my family who have known me all my life, but Paulette is one of them.

I was born in October; she was born the next May. Together with our parents and siblings we spent the vacations of our childhood wandering all over the state, and occasionally over the edges into the adjoining ones, visiting state parks and what we called tourist attractions. Our fathers worked for the same company. We bunked in the same cabins at church camp.

Mama has lots of photographs of us. In nearly every one we have our arms around each other's shoulders and our faces turned straight toward the camera, sweetly guileless, totally innocent, and proudly uninhibited. Happy children.

When we were teenagers, her dad accepted a promotion and a transfer that whisked them out of our daily lives to faraway Mississippi. I rode with them on the trip to scout out houses and it was a great adventure, the farthest west I had ever been. Still is.

The summer after my freshman year in college, there was another trek across the deepest part of the deep South so that I could be one of her bridesmaids. But before I could don my pale blue dotted-Swiss dress and wide-brimmed white hat, we had to climb through the church's bathroom window because somebody forgot the key. There is, much to our horror at the time and to our delight today, photographic evidence of breaking and entering.

After that hot June afternoon we rarely saw each other. We wore matching yellow dresses when her sister got married a few years later and visited briefly at her grandmother's eightieth birthday party, but beyond that the only contact we had was the occasional Christmas card. While I finished college and law school and came home, she settled in Louisiana, reared two boys, and helped her husband start several businesses.

Somewhere along the line they bought a place in Florida, on the Gulf side, and a few months ago, when her parents were

visiting mine and as we laughed and reminisced, I found myself
responding to a invitation to meet them there by saying, "Just tell
me when." So it was that last week I found myself heading west
on I-10 to Destin.

One of the great blessings of my life is that I have a lot of
friends. Mama likes to tell people that if I decided to make a cross-
country car trip I could stay gone a couple of months and never
have to stay in a hotel. She is probably right. The last time I
counted, I'd stayed overnight in over sixty of my friends' homes.

You learn a lot of things by doing that, the main one being
that the level of psychic comfort you feel while staying in someone
else's home is directly proportional to the depth of your
relationship. Let it be said, then, that from the moment I stepped
into the house at Destin I felt as comfortable as if I'd been at
Sandhill.

I had a lovely couple of days with Paulette's parents before
she joined us on Friday night. Saturday morning she and I, along
with her three-year-old granddaughter Macy, took a walk along
the sugar-sand beach. The late autumn sun was sharply angled
across the clear clear water that gives the Emerald Coast its name
and, despite the calendar having just turned to November,
children played in the water while their parents stretched out in
deck chairs, dozing in the sunshine.

Watching Macy chasing and being chased by the waves out of
the corners of our eyes, we strolled along the water's edge and
talked. Talked in tones that were slow and easy and cathartic.
Talked about things and people from our shared past and from
our separate presents. Talked about ourselves, where we had been
and who we had become.

That afternoon we said good-bye and promised to get
together again soon.

The photos I took on my trip, once developed, will show us, as
before, with our arms around each other's shoulders. The faces,
though, will be different. No longer guileless or innocent or
uninhibited. No longer the smooth faces of children, but the

sculpted faces of women. Women who understand that—in the midst of a world that doesn't always reward that which is authentic—one can always find a clear reflection, an undistorted image of who she is, in the mirror of a friend.

NOVEMBER 25, 2007

A few months ago Tamar was hit by a truck. Her hip was dislocated and it took the sweet and gifted folks at Saint Buddy's Hospital for Well-Beloved Animals two separate surgeries to get her pieced back together. Since then, she has been on restriction. She is not allowed to roam free and takes walks only while clipped to a long but still confining leash. She spends the majority of her days lounging on the deck.

This, I would like to make clear, was not my idea. Mama, who in a rather imperial but nonetheless understandable way has assumed full custody of Tamar, decided that she could not bear to consider the possibility of her getting hit again and Tamar has become more or less a house dog.

The other afternoon, however, Mama, Daddy, and I were standing outside chatting when a truck drove by and there was Tamar tearing across the front yard in pursuit. Daddy yelled for her to stop, but to no avail. Paradoxically fortunately, her injury and subsequent surgeries have left Tamar with a slight limp and her speed has been reduced significantly. The truck was past her long before there was any chance of a physical encounter.

She turned back toward us and obediently trotted back to the steps of the deck where she waited to be reincarcerated.

It didn't take long to discover that she'd managed to push open one of the gates that had not been completely locked and had, thus, made her escape.

Mama, all aflutter, reprimanded the still-panting dog while Daddy shook his head and mumbled, "Getting hit didn't make a bit of difference to that dog. She's still gonna chase a truck if she gets a chance."

And he is right. She will. It is who she is.

We'll never know, I suppose, why Tamar feels this untamable compulsion to throw herself into the path of large and noisy objects. Maybe she is being protective and thinks she is chasing away evil. Maybe she is competitive and thinks she has been invited to test herself. Maybe she just likes the way it feels when her heart is beating fast and her legs are pumping.

We'll never know and it doesn't really matter. Tamar is a dog who loves to chase trucks and it is one of the characteristics, along with her insatiable need to lick and her staccato bark, that make her Tamar.

Just another example of the similarities among animals, including those of us who have proportionally large brains and reasoning skills. No one of us can ever really know why anyone else is the way she is. We deceive ourselves when we assert otherwise and we disparage our relationships when we insist on trying.

"It is a fool playing God who pretends to understand everything that passes in another's heart," I read somewhere a long time ago and I've had to remind myself of that truth often as I have navigated the unpredictable and often uncharted waters of life.

Wanting to understand, pretending I do—it is such a waste of time. Better I should invest my minutes and hours and days in appreciating the uniqueness of each soul who, momentarily or permanently, imprints my heart.

One more thing about Tamar: She was completely nonplused by the effect that her brief breakout had on her humans. She just walked back over to her favorite spot, sat down, looked up, and— I promise you—smiled.

DECEMBER 9, 2007

When I asked Daddy to plant a chinaberry tree in the yard at Sandhill, he looked at me, not for the first time, as though I'd lost my mind.

"What in the world do you want with a chinaberry tree? That's the aggravatingest thing I've ever seen."

I explained to him that there is something quintessentially Southern about a chinaberry tree, that it reminds me of old farmsteads and bare feet and Sunday afternoons. I tried to get him to understand that I didn't care that the fallen berries tend to sprout into saplings almost overnight and that they stain anything with which they come in contact. I did my best to convince him that it was a good idea and, eventually, I got my tree.

In the summer, the delicate branches bloom first with long languid leaves and then hard green berries that droop from their stems with disproportionate weight and always remind me of a pawn shop sign. As the season fades, the berries themselves fade to gold and dry up light and leathery into miniature versions of deflated volleyballs.

In late fall, the berries fall to the ground and the leaves get blown away and the tree stands naked with its skinny arms stretched toward the clouds as though entreating some divine intercession to cover its embarrassment.

That's what I noticed the other morning when I stepped out on the deck to check the temperature. Silhouetted against the dull early morning sky, the tree looked small and vulnerable and not the least bit reminiscent of her summer self dancing in the warm breeze.

Behind her was the harrowed-over cornfield and beyond that the dried-out remnants of kudzu vine wrapped around the trees at the edge of the pond. The world was still and empty and colorless.

Just as I was about to go back in, I heard geese honking. From far away, probably across somebody's else farm, they were flying and calling to each other in voices faint but exquisitely clear and I realized that in the near-empty landscape of winter I could hear other things more clearly, too. Wind chimes and the call of a loon. Dogs barking and the blast of a shotgun. The scurry of an unidentified small animal through the underbrush.

I've often wondered at the reasoning behind the early Christian fathers' decision to place Christmas in this darkest, coldest part of the year. The carol calls it "the bleak midwinter." It is said that they simply wanted to piggyback on or, even better, eclipse the existing pagan celebrations that already existed, celebrations rooted in the fear that with each setting of the sun there was the possibility that it might not ever reappear.

Whatever the reason, it occurs to me that maybe one of the reasons we are called to celebrate the birth of the Christ child in the time of hibernation is that we hear better in the darkness. Without the distraction of spring's heady scents and summer's fresh tastes and autumn's riotous colors, we are left with only the sounds.

The gasp of a young girl at the sight of an angel and the angel's whisper, "Fear not." The scuffling of pilgrims down rocky roads and the harried voices of the census-takers in the tiny Palestinian towns. The whimpering of sheep, the lowing of cattle. And the first breathy cries of a newborn.

It is easy to see the stars out in the country. I can stand in my front yard, tilt my head back, and feel all my self-importance drain away. At this time of year, in the bleak midwinter, I can hear them, too. They are singing. And their song is a familiar one, the very first Christmas carol—"Glory to God in the highest, and on earth peace, goodwill toward men."

DECEMBER 23, 2007

I don't really mind eighty-degree weather in December. In fact, I'd go so far as to say that I prefer it. I can sit on the deck and read the Sunday paper. I can take the dogs rambling wearing shorts and a T-shirt. I can get out of bed without gritting my teeth in preparation for the feel of cold tile on my bare feet.

The problem with eighty-degree weather in December, however, is—as everyone was sighing last week—"It just doesn't feel like Christmas."

It was looking like Christmas, of course. Wreaths with red velvet bows. Twinkling lights. Holly and poinsettias. The ubiquitous Christmas sweater.

So it was that into the contradiction between sight and sense that I woke up last Saturday to the sound of rain hitting the windows like bird shot. On Sunday it was the wind that greeted my awakening. On Monday it was the silence of hard cold.

I stood at the door and looked outside at the frost wrapped over the landscape—in some places shiny and slick like aluminum foil, in others clear and wavy like Saran wrap. The whole world was white and pale gray and silver. Pulling my overcoat and gloves from the hall closet before rushing outside to warm up the car, I thought, "Now it feels like Christmas."

The funny thing is, of course, that most of the Christmases I've known have been nothing like iconic Currier and Ives prints. Only once can I remember snow anywhere near December 25 on the calendar. Old photographs of me and Keith and our cousins playing outside with our Christmas toys show us in nothing warmer than a sweatshirt and plenty of them show us with bare arms.

The difference between romance and reality isn't limited to weather issues. There's that whole magazine- and Food Network-encouraged delusion of the formal meal where the family dons its nicest clothes and gathers around a table set with Grandmother's china and silver and everyone comments on the deliciousness of the roasted brussels sprouts.

Does anyone arrive on the doorstep holding an armload of beautifully wrapped gifts none of which have a smooshed bow?

I think it would be lovely to have that kind of Christmas—elegant, unhurried, and draped in pristine snow—but the truth is that I would have no place in such a Christmas. I am neither elegant nor unhurried (though I am working on being both by the time I reach my dotage). My place is in a Christmas where people shaped by a life that isn't always easy, hasn't always been fair, and has forced on them grief they feel ill-prepared to carry pause long enough to realize that what matters isn't how Christmas looks, but how it feels.

And how should it feel? How did Mary and Joseph feel? How did George Washington and his army, crossing the Delaware River, feel? How did the World War I soldiers who sang with their enemies on the battlefields of Flanders during the Christmas Truce of 1914 feel? How did the crew of Apollo 8, the first humans to orbit the moon and the first to spend Christmas in space, feel?

We can only imagine, but I think they may have all felt similar things. Fear. Anticipation. Uncertainty. Awe. Because whatever happened next, whatever the results of the next few hours or days, the world would be changed forever.

Christmas changed the world forever. May we embrace that feeling and go out and do the same.

JANUARY 1, 2008

It is midnight. I walk outside onto the deck and lift my chin toward the sky full of stars. Like loose diamonds tossed across a navy blue velvet cloth in some colossal jewelry store, they take my breath away.

And when I finally release it, a tiny puff of silver floats away from my open mouth into the chilly darkness and dissolves like cotton candy.

New Year's Eve is generally pretty quiet in the country. More than once the clock has ticked (or, more accurately, the LED display has changed), moving Sandhill and the world into a new year without any notice at all. Not by me, not by the dogs, certainly not by the owl who lives in the branch behind the house or the deer whose valentine-shaped hoofprints edge the dirt road like lace. We country creatures tend to have ended our days long before the countdown begins in Times Square.

This year, though, I have made it a point to stay awake, to be conscious and thinking upon the arrival of the leap year, election year, Olympic year. I have lit lots of candles, understanding something of the uncertainty of the ancient peoples who kept a fire burning through the darkest night of the year, and have given myself over to the kind of rambling contemplation that generally leads me to the surprising conclusion that I've not been paying nearly enough attention to my life.

I try to focus on this moment. I feel the dryer-warmth pass from the towels I am folding into the palms of my hands. I breathe in the scent of almond as I rub lotion into those same hands, dry and red from all the sink-washing of the "good dishes." I stop and stare at the Christmas tree, the ornaments round and reflective, the lights a stark contrast to the darkness that has quickly covered the day.

In Wales, the winter solstice is called "the point of roughness," an idea that brings to mind the fingertips of a safe-cracker or a reader of Braille. Inflicted tenderness.

Not a particularly attractive idea in a society where easy and painless are what people want in everything from plastic surgery to divorce. To intentionally court sensitivity seems to be the height of ingratitude for the various products and mechanisms and therapies we have devised to make life easier. Which leads one to the question, "Is that what life is supposed to be? Easy?"

I am sitting at my desk now. On the edge is a wicker tray I've filled with totems, objects that remind me of where I've been, who was there with me, what I learned. A piece of red coral, a seashell, a cast-iron acorn that holds a key, a framed note card that reads, "It will all be okay in the end. If it's not okay, it's not the end."

Right outside the window, the owl swoops close enough to rustle the too-long branches on the shrubbery and opens his mouth to the long mournful cry I have grown to love.

Time passes. Two hours until midnight. One hour until midnight. Thirty minutes. Five minutes. Ten seconds.

"Five ... four ... three ..." the voice on the radio whispers into the microphone on the stage of the Ryman Auditorium in Nashville. "Two ... one ... Happy New Year."

It is midnight. I walk outside onto the deck and lift my chin toward the sky full of stars. I hold myself tightly against the chill. A new year. I take a deep breath and raise a glass to whatever is out there. Easy or not.

JANUARY 20, 2008

For years now Daddy has struggled to keep unobstructed the spring that feeds the pond from which he pumps irrigation water. In the course of one night, beavers can build—and have built on several occasions—a formidable dam that nothing will bust loose save several hours of ax-wielding. Every winter he spends an afternoon or two hunched against the wind, freeing the spring of its obstruction.

Just the other day Mama was relating to some visiting friends this less-than-bucolic aspect of country living. While listening to the story of how Jake the Wonder Dog swam to the middle of the pond, subdued one of the interloping varmints, and then amazingly made the necessary mathematical calculation to determine the shortest route back to land, one of the friends noticed an incredible example of the beavers' handiwork.

At the edge of the pond was a pine tree, as big around as a grown man's thigh, that had been completely eaten through by the resident rodents. What was so remarkable was that the tree had not fallen. It stood suspended in mid-air, levitating directly above the stump from which it had been amputated.

A quick glance confirmed that the law of gravity had not been repealed and that, in fact, the branches of the tree were entwined with those of another tree. The embrace of its neighbor kept it standing.

The reason those friends were visiting was to attend a wedding—their own. In a few short days, they and those who love them had put together the arrangements for a ceremony to be held on the front porch of Sandhill and on Sunday afternoon, as the wind chimes sang and the breeze licked at loose tendrils of hair and the hems of flirty dresses, they held hands and exchanged rings and promised to stay together forever.

"What greater joy," the judge asked the two of them and all of us who listened, "is there for two human souls than to join together to strengthen each other in all their endeavors, to support each other through all sorrow, and to share with each other in all gladness?

"Love is stronger than your conflicts, bigger than life's changes. Love is the miracle always inviting you to learn, to blossom, to expand. It is to love that you must always return.

"You are about to make vows and promises to each other. Today, these vows are beautiful words representing even more beautiful intentions. My prayer for you is that as you live these vows over the years, the meaning of these words will deepen and the happy times of your life will be twice as joyous because you'll be sharing them with someone you love. And when life gets tough, it will only be half as hard because there is someone by your side to help carry the burden."

Watching their faces, I couldn't help thinking about that tree, the one the beavers had chewed and gnawed and torn asunder. It had done nothing to invite the attack, nothing to encourage the assault, nothing to threaten its assailant and, yet, it very nearly found itself felled.

Most of the troubles that come our way are not the result of anything wrong we have done, anything important we have failed to do. They are simply the result of living in what the theologians call a fallen world. Bad things happen to good people, beavers cut down trees. What keeps them standing, the people and the trees, is being close enough to allow those nearby to bear some of the load.

I think, maybe, that that is as good a definition of marriage as anything I've ever heard: two people standing close enough to each other to share the load.

FEBRUARY 3, 2008

Already the days are getting longer. The darkest days of winter are past and the sun is lingering on the horizon like a lover saying a reluctant good-bye.

Yesterday afternoon I got home a little early. After reading the mail and starting a load of laundry, I took my book out to the front porch to absorb the tender luminance of sunset. I read the words, turned the pages, but my thoughts were divided—half of them inside the story, half of them dwelling on the telephone call that had come, a few hours earlier, so unexpectedly.

"Are you by yourself?" Mama had asked in a voice that was clearly struggling against the rise of tears in her throat.

From down the hall came the voices of my coworkers and the high-pitched drone of machines. Telephones were ringing, printers were humming like helicopters about to take off. The sounds of busyness. The sounds of distraction. The sounds of an ordinary day.

Sounds that, with the question mark in my mother's voice, went silent. It was as though the mute button on some previously unknown remote control had been pressed by the finger of God.

The news, of course, was not good. Our dear family friend, a man who grew up with Daddy and whose children grew up with me and Keith, had died. Suddenly. He and his wife had been trying for years to get Mama and Daddy to visit them in Florida. Had teased, cajoled, bribed. Had even pulled me into the fray by getting me to promise to drive them.

But it hadn't happened. The last time we'd tried was in October, but corn had to be cut and a weather change was on the way and when the time came to go, I went by myself.

"Why," Mama had whimpered, "do we put things off?"

I watched the angle of the sun's light change, the shadows across the porch grow sharper. The rocking chair, arcing back in response to my push, forward in response to my letting go, eased my anxious heart into a gentle rhythm. The rush of feelings that had pounded me like the rising tide died down as the flow began its unavoidable and imperceptible turn.

Why do we put things off? Why do we, as Stephen Covey puts it, elevate the urgent over the important?

Regret may well be the most painful of emotions because it is self-inflicted. Grief and anger, joy and excitement, they all spring from points outside the self; regret has only one source. And because we expect more from ourselves than we would ever expect from anyone else, we refuse the only cure, medicine that we easily spoon out to others—a teaspoon of forgiveness, a dose of second chance.

This is what I remember about Mr. John—that he always called Daddy "Cuz," that he never seemed to mind when we played touch football in the front yard and he got all the girls on his team, and that he loved to tell stories, a characteristic that on its own was enough to make me love him.

And I remember that the last time I was with him he told me how proud he was of me, something you never get too old to hear.

I have tried to live my life without regret. I've not been completely successful. Fortunately, the people I have failed still love me and because of that I get the opportunity every day to show them how grateful I am for the second chance.

That, as much as the love itself, may well be the greatest gift of all.

FEBRUARY 17, 2008

I was reading about water bears the other day. They are microscopic creatures that look like tiny little bears with eight legs; their scientific name, tardigrada, means "slow mover." They can live for up to fifty years and at temperatures as low as -400 degrees Fahrenheit. If the water in which they live dries up, they go into a state of hibernation called cryptobiosis, "hidden life."

It was hard not to make a comparison between the water bears and people. They have eight legs, but move slowly. We have two legs and, most of the time, move too swiftly for our spirits to keep up. We generally live longer, but our range of liveable temperatures is so small that we find it necessary to destroy much of the natural environment to produce fuel for the heating and cooling of our buildings.

The only thing, it appeared from my reading, that we large mammals with the abilities to reason and elaborately verbally communicate have in common with the invisible water bears is that hidden life.

Call it hibernation or cryptobiosis or privacy, the reality is that when our water dries up, when the environment in which we have thrived is suddenly and irrevocably changed, it is the nature of men and women to shut down, close up shop, board up the windows and make sure that those around us see the sign on the door that says, in big block letters, "Do not disturb!"

When I was in Girl Scouts part of what we had to learn to earn the First Aid badge was how to treat shock. To be honest, I don't remember much beyond the elevated feet and warm blanket parts. Gratefully, I never had to use that knowledge, but it bothers me a little that the instruction was limited to responding to physical shock.

No one, not the Girl Scouts or my Sunday School teachers or youth group leaders or, later, my psychology professors, offered any instruction at all on how to address emotional shock, the feeling of numbness that engulfs you when the world cracks and dissolves into a million tiny shards of glass. The petrification of all thought, the inability to make even the smallest decision.

The truth is that there is no stop-drop-and-roll prescription for that kind of catastrophe. No acronym to remind you of the steps to take to make everything right again. No instructions that, if followed, guarantee a return to normalcy.

Like the water bears, we humans react without thought, with only instinct: We draw ourselves in and wait.

When the water bears are in the dormant state, they are as light as dust particles and a breeze can pick them up, toss them around and deposit them somewhere else. No resistance, no questioning. Yielded to the wind, sailing through the sky, eventually landing in a new place, a place where the water puddles or streams or falls from the clouds in syrupy drops. A place where the hidden life ends and the real life resumes.

Last week as I stood at the altar and received the ashes on my forehead, I was struck, as always, by the fragility of life. We are so vulnerable. Naked we come into the world, naked we leave and, in between, if we are to experience anything of love or joy or contentment, we must remain naked, exposed to the elements, exposed to each other.

There is always the chance that the water will dry up. Drought. Evaporation. The thirst of a passing dog. But when it does, when the unbidden and unwanted change occurs, it is good to remember the water bear who allows himself to become still and quiet and light as air.

It is good to remember that a breath of wind is coming. It will lift you off the dry and empty ground and drop you gently in a pool of water where the hidden life will thaw, where the boards will come off the windows and where the sunshine can trickle in.

I have a new friend. A mockingbird has taken to arriving at Sandhill early every morning to perch on the empty shepherd's crook standing at the edge of the deck. Balanced carefully on the cold curve of iron, beak tilted into the crisp morning air, he looks for all the world like a well-fed vassal surveying his fiefdom. Or better, with his pale gray feathers that end in a long square tail, like a British bridegroom in cutaway and ascot.

He is an attractive bird, but he seems to have frightened away all the wrens, the sparrows, the cardinals, and the jays that normally flit and flutter from one bare branch to another, cheeping and chirping and singing the sun up.

Leaning against the sill, staring at the proud bird in his stillness and solitude, it is inevitable that I remember Harper Lee's Scout Finch and her lawyer daddy whose plain goodness was one of the things that led me to my profession. When Atticus gives Scout an air rifle it is with the admonition that "it's a sin to kill a mockingbird." Scout takes her confusion about her father's words to an older neighbor, who explains: "Mockingbirds don't do one thing but make music for us to enjoy. They don't eat up people's gardens, don't nest in corncribs, they don't do one thing but sing their hearts out for us. That's why it's a sin to kill a mockingbird."

Scout Finch lives in a world stained with hypocrisy and cruelty and selfishness. But she doesn't know that. Not yet. Not until she sits in a courtroom balcony and watches her father confront, unsuccessfully it turns out, those marauders.

Wandering off into the woods of thought, I pick up the well-worn trail that leads me to my own courtroom balcony, the place where I first found myself wrestling with the intrusion of pain and disillusionment into a previously halcyon world. Things—I learned, we all learn eventually—are not as they should be.

Volcanos and wars erupt. Poverty and rumors spread. Children and dreams die. The best that even the wisest among us can offer is platitude, not explanation. Is it any wonder that a malignant heart so rarely raises us to righteous indignation anymore?

It is still a sin to kill a mockingbird, to harm the harmless, but unless it is our mockingbird in our backyard most of us are too jaded and resigned to care.

But back in the balcony of the courthouse in Maycomb, Alabama, as a defeated Atticus slowly gathers his things and turns to leave the courtroom, Rev. Sykes touches Scout's shoulder and whispers, "Miss Jean Louise, stand up. Your father's passin'."

In that moment, Scout begins to see that the world in which she lives, the one stained with hypocrisy and cruelty and selfishness, is also colored with generosity and loyalty and love. She begins to understand that even as she must shield herself against evil, she must open herself to good.

I've noticed that my mockingbird doesn't sing. He doesn't chirp and cheep. He doesn't imitate the songs of his cousins, loudly and repetitively. Not once has he parted his beak, puffed up his throat, expelled his breath, and offered a song.

If I measured his worth on Miss Maudie's scale, I guess I'd be justified in at least shooing, if not shooting, him.

I watch him a while longer, notice the way his wings unfold like a lady's fan when he loops over to the lowest limb of the chinaberry tree, how the white tips reflect the sunlight like snow, and it occurs to me that maybe, just maybe, the greater sin, the transgression worse than killing a mockingbird, might be trying to make him something he isn't, not loving him for what he is.

MARCH 16, 2008

The best gift is one that is unexpected or one that is particularly suited to the recipient. When a single gift is both it makes the heart sing.

This past Sunday I was walking with a friend down the long wide beach on Jekyll Island. There were few others out in the breezy afternoon—a middle-aged couple walking five lean and leggy greyhounds and a handful of birdwatchers who, when asked what they were hoping to see, replied, "Anything that flies."

The sky was flat and the palest of blues. The tide had ebbed, leaving an unusual number of horseshoe crab shells and the usual surfeit of trembling jellyfish scattered across the sand. Cumberland Island, just a few miles south, seemed almost touchable in the clear spring light.

We headed south intending to meet up with Judy, my friend's friend, a transplanted Californian with a specific passion for horses and a general appreciation of all things outdoors. As we walked, we talked of ordinary things—her cats, my dog, road trips we might take one day, the fact that I'd forgotten to put on sunscreen.

We caught up with Judy at the southernmost part of the island where a school of dolphins was churning up the water like an old-fashioned eggbeater. Diving and rolling and circling each other like children playing chase, the dolphins moved as a group, with the current, oblivious to their role as entertainers to the people onshore.

"I found something for you," Judy told me and strode up the dunes where she had left the treasure. She came back with a perfect conch shell. Complete. Unbroken. I'd never seen one so unblemished, so whole. At least not outside a shell shop.

Sand clung to the winding spires of the ocean-scarred outside. Inside, the shell was glassy smooth and pink like lip gloss. It filled my hand exactly.

Judy explained that she'd seen just a little of it sticking out of the sand and that, when she started digging and realized how deeply it was buried, she suspected it might be whole. "The further down in the sand it's buried," she told us, "the better chance there is that it's unbroken."

When I got home I put my shell up on the mantel at the foot of some candlesticks. There were a handful of other shells already there—a couple of palm-sized scallops, another conch, all of them half- or quarter-shells only, all of them missing parts of themselves. And I remembered what Judy had said about being buried.

Is it possible that the only way to stay whole is to stay buried? And is staying buried any way to live? The truth is that my conch shell—without any cracks, without any holes, without any absent pieces—was empty. The snail that had lived there had been washed out by the ocean's waves or eaten in somebody's fritter. The container was still beautiful, but the life was gone.

Last week the news was full of the senseless, heartbreaking deaths of two young women—popular college students, good citizens, well-loved daughters. In each case there was a question about what she was doing in a particular place at a particular time. A reasonable question. An unavoidable question. And, ultimately, probably an unanswerable question.

I have another question: Had either of the beautiful coeds been somewhere else, would she have been guaranteed another day? Had either spent all her days on a security-camera'ed, razor-wired, soldier-guarded campus, would she have been protected from all the evil that resides in the world? Had either stayed buried in the sand she would have been just like my conch shell—beautiful, unbroken, and empty.

Life is about opportunity and risk. Life is about the willingness to open the mind and the heart. Life is about being filled with generosity and curiosity and love. Life is not an empty shell.

MARCH 30, 2008

Mama didn't teach me to cook. Whatever I know of following recipes, cleaning up as you go, and seasoning to taste, I learned from other sources.

What she did teach me was to stitch a hem so delicate as to be invisible and so strong as to be unravelable, to set in a sleeve with no puckers, and to lay out a pattern with no waste of fabric. She taught me how to figure yardage, how to match thread, how to make a dart, a pleat, and a tuck, and how to put on a waistband.

By the time I entered the eighth grade home ec lab I was earning spending money by helping Mama who, as we used to say, took in sewing. I steam pressed the seams and put in the hems of the dresses and coats and blouses she made for the ladies who, for some reason I could not fathom at the time, preferred homemade clothes to the ones hanging in the windows at Henry's and Tilli's and Belk.

I was, then, most resentful of Miss Williams's requirement that I use tracing paper to mark seam lines. Any idiot, it seemed to me, ought to be able to hold the fabric against the seam guide and stitch a straight line. I also couldn't understand why she would want me to make an apron when, heaven's to Betsy, I'd mastered that three years before in fifth grade 4-H.

I eventually won that battle and while everyone else was trying to figure out how to make their apron gathers uniform, I was obnoxiously trimming the facing on the neck of my dress and imagining how cool it was that my project was actually going to see use whereas my classmates' would most likely end up stuffed into their bottom dresser drawers.

It would be years, of course, before I grasped the real value of what I had learned, literally, at my mother's feet. Infinitely more satisfying than being able to say "I made it myself," is being able—as result of what my mother taught me—to recognize quality workmanship, an ability that transfers far beyond the walls of a clothing store and into more intangible endeavors. Unrolling a piece of fabric from a bolt and crushing a corner of it to test its hand is a good metaphor for determining the sincerity of a relationship. Matching plaids is akin to finding the right job or neighborhood or mate.

Even the terminology of sewing teaches lessons: Selvage and bias conjure up vivid images of the contrast between flexibility and rigidity. Seam allowance and presser foot and tension knob speak to the necessity, not just the unavoidability, of structure and rules.

All of which may be why no one learns to sew anymore. It requires time. It requires discipline. It requires stillness, quietness, and concentration, all of which are commodities in short supply in a world where we drink instant coffee, send instant messages, and long to be instant winners.

It's been a long time since I laid out my last pattern, put in my last zipper, or threaded my last bobbin. I suspect that the motor belt on my sewing machine, not taken out of its case in years, has rotted through. There are moments, though, when I need to be reminded of all I learned watching Mama hunched over her Singer, its own peculiar song caught by the breeze through the open window and suffused into the summer night. And in those moments I find myself being drawn into a store that still has an aisle marked notions.

I take a deep breath and run my fingers over the rainbow of Coats and Clark spools, spin the button rack, flip through a few pages of the Simplicity pattern book and, in no longer than it takes to thread a needle, I am myself again, instinctively stitching together the rough-edge pattern pieces of my life with a perfect five-eighths inch seam.

One day last week, during one of the more temperate—though brief—moments in what has been a rather schizophrenic weather pattern, I went out on the deck to read. There were probably ten or twelve different birdcalls echoing in the branch and the wind chimes were tink-tink-tinking from the lowest limb of the chinaberry tree.

The sound that drowned them all out, the sound that with its nearness and potential for danger demanded attention, was the drone of a single bumblebee. I had hardly settled back on the chaise when the demon appeared out of the waxy green branches of the ligustrum bush at the corner of the house and came to hover about six inches from the tip of my nose.

Making the quick decision that immobility might translate into invisibility, I held my breath and stared at the fat little insect whose wings were nothing more than a silver blur against the blue sky. Fortunately for me, I was soon determined to be a non-pollen-producing organism and the bee buzzed away.

There were a couple more fly-by's, but for the most part we ignored each other, each of us intent on gathering its own form of nectar.

I don't have any specific memory of learning the childhood rules of insects, but at some point someone must have told me that, first, if you don't bother the bee, the bee won't bother you and, second, if the bee does sting you he will immediately die. I accepted as truth those statements as every child accepts as truth the pronouncements of bigger people.

It was quite a coincidence—if there is such a thing—that, just a few days after my nod-and-bob cocktail party encounter with the bee, I had my folkloric knowledge both confirmed and refuted as good science. The regular old South Georgia bumblebee is, as I had learned, an exclusively defensive stinger, but the "one sting and then death" proposition applies only to its cousin the honeybee.

"They attack when threatened, but only as a last defense," the author of my book wrote. "With the injection, their stinger and venom sac are ripped from their body and they die."

Given my propensity for seeing everything as metaphor, I was immediately struck by the "only as a last defense" part and felt my heart swelling for the little critters, both the honeybees and we people who behave in the very same way.

Except that—let's be honest here—we people tend to leave off that last subordinate clause. We just attack when threatened. Your ability to make it to the meeting in time is jeopardized by the car merging into traffic, so you blow your horn, maybe even give your middle finger a little exercise. The customer service representative on the other end of the telephone line doesn't seem to want to help me, so I start using what I hope are intimidating lawyer words. The first-grader's Crayon pack is missing the yellow one she wants, so she breaks the red one in two.

It's sad. There is really very little that threatens the twenty-first-century American. Nearly all of us have plenty of food. There are no bands of guerrillas haunting our subdivisions. Most of the diseases that killed our great-grandparents have been eradicated or held in check by medicine. Yet we behave as though we are hapless honeybees.

Sadder still is all that is ripped from our souls when we recklessly respond. Dignity, peace of mind, clarity of conscience—attributes that require patient cultivation, character traits that take years to develop and only seconds to destroy. Virtues without which the nobility of the human spirit will die.

You'd think we were smarter than honeybees. Maybe not.

APRIL 27, 2008

I am standing on the loggia, two stories tall with a domed stone roof. The wide marble steps lead down to a fountain that sprays millions of water-drop mirrors into the warm spring afternoon. Black wrought-iron streetlights and gnarly gray oaks, a hundred years old at least, line the driveway and beds of just-bloomed pansies splotch the wide green lawn.

A person can have more than one home and I have left one to come to another. I have left Sandhill to come to Wesleyan.

It has been thirty years since I accepted my real sheepskin diploma and carefully moved the purple and white tassel to the other side of my mortarboard. Thirty years since I said goodbye to this place, but, being a good daughter, I have punctuated that thirty years with frequent visits and careful attention. I look around and it is as if I never left.

Soon I am roused from my reverie by the screeching and hugging and touching of arriving classmates. I am so glad to be the first one here. So glad to do the welcoming.

There are huge smiles that look absolutely no different from the ones I remember except for the tiny lines that form at the corners of their eyes, lines that look nothing like crows' feet and everything like sunbursts.

Each of these women has moved her own personal heaven and earth to be here, to be in what is—to us at least—a sacred place, a cathedral of red brick and arched doorways and marble columns. A place where we sang the hymns and recited the creeds and fulfilled the prophecies that said, "This is who you will be."

On Saturday night, after all the formal events—the board elections and award presentations and campus tours—we gather at the home of one of our classmates. The backyard is lit with candlelight that softens the edges of everything, including our aging faces. A handful of us gather around a table to catch up, to exchange stories.

One of the Janets tells us how she made her way back to the love of her life thirty years after meeting him for the first time, how she inherited his daughter as her own, and how, yes, she did think she would burst with pride as, just that morning, she had helped induct that daughter into the Wesleyan Alumnae Association. We are all beaming. Starbursts are at the corners of our eyes again.

And it is at that moment that I understand. Understand that we come back home for the stories. We come back to tell our own and to hear those of our sisters. Because it is in the telling and in the hearing that each of us learns this great truth: There is only one story—the story of birth and growth, of struggle and loss, of transformation and redemption.

In a few hours I, we will be headed to our other homes. I, we will pick up where we left off, open the book at the bookmark and begin again. I take one last look at the sweet sweet faces of the girls I have watched become women and this is what I think: They knew me at seventeen and now, at three times that, it becomes clear that they still do.

It is a rare comfort in a world we treat as though it was disposable to come across something that remains, that persists, that stays. Within the arms of my alma mater, my "nourishing mother," I have found such a thing. It is the truth of story and the authentic life that results from its telling.

MAY 11, 2008

Collin is six years old. He has eyes like malted milk balls—round and chocolate brown. He picked up a book from the library table and, following the instructions of the librarian to "Go over there and let that lady read you your book," walked the few steps to where I was sitting and sat down beside me.

"What's your name?" I asked.

"Collin," he answered. "She wrote it right here in the front of my book." He pointed to the perfectly printed name his teacher had written under the RIF stamp on the inside front cover of *The Dinosaur Who Lived In My Backyard.*

He then volunteered his last name and when I, thinking I might know his parents, asked their names, he squinted those luminous eyes, stared off into the distance for a moment and said, "My dad's name is Daddy. And my mom's name is Mama."

Well, of course.

Collin told me he was in kindergarten. I had to smile. Is there anything more winsome than a kindergartener? Anything more gripping than the openness of that face, the generosity of that smile?

The day of Adam's kindergarten orientation, he and I left his mom in the classroom talking to the teacher. We had taken only a few steps down the hall when he stopped, still holding my hand, and said, "Kap, I don't think I know enough to go to kindergarten."

My heart clutched. I want to grab him up and run all the way back to the farm, to secret him away from all the hard and unexplainable things that I knew he would have to endure once he embarked on this existence outside the security of his family's arms.

I've always thought it most noble and courageous and, well, mature of me that I didn't. Instead, I told him, "Oh, I think you do.

All you need to know to go to kindergarten is your name and your teacher's name and how to get to your classroom."

The blue eyes, fixated on my face, were tentative, unsure.

"So," I offered, "what is your name?"

"Adam Bradley."

"And what is your teacher's name?"

"Miss Akins."

"Good. Now let's go out to the front where I'll drop you off in the morning and you can show me how to get back to your room."

We started at the sidewalk where the carpool lines formed, walked down the long breezeway to the kindergarten wing, took a left, and followed the circular hallway to the room where the door was decorated with a cartoon alligator.

He pointed.

"Yes!" I practically screamed. "You did it! See? I knew that you knew enough to go to kindergarten."

Relief showed itself in the slightest upward curve of the corners of his mouth, what—for the usually taciturn Adam—amounted to a smile.

It is not an easy thing to be an adult who loves, who adores a child. It is not easy to watch while he marches off to a place you've never been or to listen while she talks about people you've never met. It is not easy to acknowledge, even in the smallest way, the separateness of this being whose breath seems to be your own.

Collin, if he's anything like my Adam, will probably have little to say about his field trip when he is asked about his day by parents who soak up each word like intravenous nourishment. Two weeks from now he will not remember the name of his book or that a lady read it to him. But I will remember enough for both of us.

As the teacher called the children to line up to leave, I stood and patted Collin on the shoulder. "It was nice to meet you," I told him.

He smiled. And then, tossing the words over his shoulder as though they were birdseed, not gold doubloons, he said, "Maybe I will see you again."

I hope so, Collin. I hope so.

MAY 25, 2008

Add two cups sugar to two cups fresh blackberries. Stir over medium heat for fifteen to twenty minutes. Cool.

So I did. I stood at the stove, stirring and stirring and stirring, watching the bumpy black berries soften and burst, coloring the sugar the shade of a deep bruise. As the juice ran and turned the sugar into syrup, the stirring got smoother and a little monotonous.

It is highly likely that I could have left the jam for a moment or two—to answer the phone or move wet clothes from the washer to the dryer or check the score of the Braves game—without making any difference in the finished product, but there was something about the directness and simplicity of the instructions that called me to diligence. I would, as directed, stir for fifteen to twenty minutes.

The rhythm of the stirring and the observation of the near-alchemy that was taking place before my eyes coaxed me into thinking about a lot of things. I thought about how much easier it would have been to simply buy blackberry jam (a thought I quickly dismissed by remembering the difference between Mama's creamed corn and that produced by the Green Giant).

I thought about the array of scratches all over my arms and legs that had resulted from my blackberry foraging. I thought about how accomplished I would feel once the jam had been spooned into the tiny Ball jars with the fruit-embellished lids. And I thought about the friends and family with whom I would share.

I watched my wrist rotate with the turn of the spatula, watched the tornado-like swirling in the bottom of the pot, watched the liquid slosh up in broad waves like purple ric-rac. And, staring into the soon-to-be jam, the thoughts turned to images.

I saw Mama standing at the counter slicing up cucumbers that would become pickles. I heard the whistle and jingle of the pressure cooker and the rip of corn shucks being stripped from their ears. I smelled the greenness of beans just snapped. I felt under my thumbnails the tenderness of an afternoon's pea-shelling.

And there I was, ten years old and not-so-quietly stewing over what I saw as an imposition on my summer. Sitting under a tree in a folding aluminum lawn chair, balancing in my lap a blue plastic hospital pan, running my fingers through shell after shell of peas and listening to Mama and Grannie and an assemblage of aunts and cousins talk about people whose names I did not recognize but who, I was assured, were kin to me.

I wanted to be inside, stretched out on my bed with the window fan blowing straight into my face, a Nancy Drew book in my hands. It was in that world, the world of daring adventures and unsolved mysteries, that I belonged. Not in the one where ordinary people did ordinary things. Shelling peas and picking off peanuts would not get me closer to the exotic life that I was certain was meant to be mine.

The timer on the stove went off and ended my reverie. The fifteen minutes was up. I turned off the stove and moved the pot to another burner for the last step of the process: Cool.

Remembering the frustration of those sweltering summer days, it occurred to me that making my self has been a little like making blackberry jam. At ten, I was a combination of wildness and sweetness and life would have to do quite a bit of heating and stirring before the two things melded into something that was worth sharing, something that would keep.

The girl who so wanted to discover a hidden staircase, receive a mysterious letter, or locate a message in a hollow oak would find that real secrets are far less tangible. The girl who wanted to catch a nefarious criminal on a dude ranch would learn that the bad guys are rarely identifiable by their outward appearances. The girl who imagined a place worth exploring only as a place far, far away would uncover, within herself, the grandest tel of all.

I could not resist sticking my finger into the warming purple goo. I opened my mouth and closed my lips over the sticky sweetness. Oh, Nancy Drew, did you ever slow down long enough to make blackberry jam?

JUNE 8, 2008

The water wasn't just one color of blue. It was every color of blue. It was the whole blue section of the original Crayola 64—periwinkle and aquamarine, cornflower and blue green, green blue and turquoise blue.

And it was clear. So clear that I could see sandbars floating just beneath the surface as far as a hundred yards away. Tiny underwater islands that made me think of Atlantis.

The sensation of water on both sides of the road was unsettling and I turned my head from side to side, trying to imagine how you measure the tides in such a place. The top was down and I could feel the midday sun radiating through the skin on my arms and legs. The wind snatched at my hair, tugging at random strands as though to lift me straight into the sky like a reverse-image Rapunzel.

And then came the bridge. Seven miles long. Flat and straight and narrow, a seam down the middle of the channel that connects the Gulf of Mexico and the Florida Strait. The crayon-colored water was under our feet now, under the levitating asphalt held just out of its reach by concrete pillars. From any direction the view was the same—water stretching to the horizon and melting into sky. Layers and layers of blue.

I'd not really expected this sensual assault. The road trip to Key West was a means to an end: There, at the literal end of the continental United States, I would see my Kate for the first time in a year. I was eager and anxious and wound as tight as Dick's hatband.

Somewhere around Big Pine Key, I think, I gave in. Stopped trying to download like digital photos every image that fell on my retinas. Relaxed my shoulders and let the light and warmth swallow me up. By the time the tires hit the bridge, time didn't matter.

I spent four days in Key West. Kate was a generous and indulgent tour guide. She took me to the Hemingway House and the Robert Frost Cottage. She let me take her picture inside the Butterfly Conservatory and at the "southernmost point" monument. She took me to Mallory Square to see the sunset and ignored my obvious amazement at all the things I saw on Duval Street.

When the time for goodbyes came, I squeezed her tight, reminded her of my love, and watched her drive off in the car she'd bought without any help to the job she'd gotten without any help. And I didn't cry.

I was so proud of myself.

Later, several weeks later, this morning as a matter of fact, I finally grasped what my heart had been trying to teach my head. And it wasn't, as I might have guessed, that the journey itself is at least as important as the destination.

The point of all that endless blue water and the indelible image it left on my memory was this: The magic of the journey is directly proportional to the pilgrim's passion for the destination.

I had packed my bags and loaded the car with only one end in mind: Kate, my Kate. A year's holidays had come and gone without her presence. Four times the seasons at Sandhill had changed without her seeing them. Hundreds of sunsets had followed sunrises without her opening the back door and heading to the refrigerator for a Capri Sun.

It was hunger I felt: hunger for the light of her smile, the lilt of her voice, the feel of her half-hug. It was hunger that drove me seven hundred miles. It was hunger that rubbed me sandpaper-raw and opened my eyes to the lessons and the loveliness of the road.

JUNE 22, 2008

Ancient maps often labeled uncharted, unexplored regions with the simple phrase: "Where Dragons Lie."

Last night, needing to think, needing to mull over, chew on, process the events of the last few days, I sat on the deck and watched the light fade. The sun had vanished beneath the horizon and the sky was washed in the pale chic pastels of a Pottery Barn nursery. There was a breeze coming from the east and the windcatcher, a pendulum hanging from the center of the wind chimes, whirled like a dervish in a tight spiral. The high-pitched bell song echoed out into the branch, a small stone making ripples in a small pond.

Where Dragons Lie.

I had just watched, at the suggestion of a friend, a science fiction television show in which a planet was discovered on which life could be maintained only inside a dome. The air and water quality outside had been so contaminated by centuries of industrial growth that life could not be maintained there; the people living in the dome, however, were content. Outside the dome, the area beyond which their maps had been drawn, was of no consequence to them. But, unknown to them, the dome was shrinking.

Where Dragons Lie.

Out of the corner of my eye I could see a jagged streak of heat lightning, bright orange like a HAZMAT suit. A mockingbird glided through the carport and came to rest on the deck rail, stayed long enough to make sure that I knew he was ignoring me, and flew away. I noticed that the lavender I had grown from seed was a little taller, that the zinnias were healthy, that one of the hummingbird feeders would need more food soon.

The crickets and frogs began singing and I realized that I'd not done much thinking, mulling, or chewing. Realized that as the day had wound down around me, gotten slower, gotten cooler, gotten quieter, so had my thoughts. And in the quietness I realized that the answer to my dilemma lay at the edges of the map.

We are the cartographers of our own lives. We are handed a compass, a quill, and a few sheets of parchment and told to "Go."

For much of my life I carried mine around in a field jacket and spent my time navigating by the maps that others had made. I picked up those maps at school and at church, at Girl Scouts and summer camp. I tore them out of books and magazines. I picked up several pockets full from my family. And, for the most part, I had a pretty good time. I saw lots of tourist attractions, read lots of historical markers, had my picture made in front of a lot of monuments.

But one day, while stuffing yet another ticket stub into my pocket, I found the compass. Lying in the palm of my hand, its needle quivered and so did my heart. With no hesitation, I threw away the others' maps and set out.

I could have stayed. I could have continued building my dome, making it self-sufficient, brain-washing myself into believing that the curve above my head was real sky, but eventually the dome would have started shrinking and so would I.

Some people are born running toward the edge, ready to explore and excavate. Most of us aren't. Most of us believe in dragons.

I felt a bug bite of some kind and knew it was time to go inside. One more glance around the night landscape. One more deep breath of midsummer air. One more sigh of gratitude for the compass that pointed the way to where dragons lie.

JULY 6, 2008

The rabbit wasn't large—bigger than a bunny, but not full grown. It sat among the palmetto scrubs and wiregrass along the edge of the road. Jake and I noticed it at the same time.

Jake is Adam's dog, a thick-muscled golden Lab with a serious face. He is smart, one of those dogs with whom you tend to carry on a conversation and half-expect to get an answer back. He was my only companion that afternoon. We'd been up the road a mile or so and were headed home when the rabbit showed up.

In a matter of seconds Jake had left the road, leapt over the ditch, and hit the ground running on the overgrown timber trail that runs parallel to the road. "Jake!" I called out sharply. "Jake!" His long yellow legs kept galloping toward the white puff of tail that bounced ahead of him.

The rabbit had a head start and, moving surprisingly quickly on short stumpy legs, disappeared into the brush—sort of a reverse magician's trick. Jake came up short, his nose quivering just above the ground at the hole into which the rabbit had dived.

"Jake!"

He lifted his head and quizzically tilted it toward me and the road. "Leave that rabbit alone!"

One more look at the hole. One more look at me. A soft—I promise you—sigh and then retreat. He jumped back over the ditch and trotted back up to me. "Good boy, Jake. Good boy."

To be honest, I was more than a little surprised that Jake abandoned his pursuit of the rabbit. He is, after all, a dog and dogs chase rabbits. It is instinctual and, as we often tell ourselves in defense of actions of which we are regretful but for which we have no explanation, you can't fight instinct.

Except that, apparently, based upon what I'd just seen, you can.

In that moment Jake, who isn't supposed to have a moral code, made a choice. Instead of responding to the adrenaline that made his heart race, that made his fur stand up, that sent him running madly after something that wasn't anywhere close to a physical match for him, he responded instead to my voice.

Jake knows me. I feed him when he wanders down to my house. I offer him a big bowl of water after we've been walking. I scruff his ears and talk to him in that strange voice we humans reserve for babies and animals. I love Jake. And he loves me back.

And so he comes when I call.

A triumph of love over instinct.

I thought about all that as Jake and I walked on down the big hill and back up the rise toward home and I realized that Jake's choice was the one that we are asked to make every day, many times a day. We are asked to respond to all sorts of stimuli, everything from the car that brakes suddenly in front of us to the telephone call that brings bad news.

We are asked to respond and we always have to choose. Instinct or love.

Sometimes the response is instantaneous, without conscious deliberation, but most of the time—in a world where "fight or flight" is not a literal confrontation—there is plenty of time to consider the ramifications of choice. And in that time, the moments or days or years that flow by between stimulus and response, we get to decide whether we will respond out of self-preservation or self-sacrifice.

Instinct or love. Jake understands that. I hope I do.

JULY 20, 2008

Filtered by summer fog, the sun—almost halfway up the sky at 7:30—was a flat white disk, a poker chip dropped by an inattentive gambler.

I heaved my briefcase into the passenger seat of the car, buckled my seat belt, and turned the key, the sequence of rote motions that sets the rhythm of my life five days a week. Lifting my eyes to the rearview mirror in preparation for backing out of the carport, my mind already racing through the list of tasks that awaited me, I felt the startle before I realized what I had seen.

Directly in front of me, stretching from one of the deck posts to the arm of one of the chairs was a spiderweb, at least a foot and a half across, dangling from the thinnest of supporting threads.

The diffused sunlight silhouetted every one of its strands glistening like icicles. It quivered in a breeze so slight that I hadn't felt it when I'd walked out into the damp morning. I couldn't move. Just stared for a few seconds like a hypnotist's fool.

When I felt my heart beating again, I unbuckled the seat belt, got out of the car and walked carefully—tiptoed really, almost like walking into a church—up the steps of the deck and over to the web, kneeling down to stare into the gauzy labyrinth.

Surrounded by uncommon quietness—the morning birds having sensed, it seemed, that silence was the only psalm needed—I counted the sections, twenty-three pieces of spiderweb pie, each seam etched with beads of dew smaller than pinheads, tremulous and hesitant but never falling. I looked for the weaver, but saw no sign of the creature that had spent the entire night spinning.

Anonymity is not something to which many of us aspire. We want to be known in a deep and soulful way by those we love, but we want more. We want to be known by strangers, by people whose faces are caricatures, whose voices are nothing more than vibrations on our eardrums.

A significant portion of American children who are asked, "What do you want to be when you grow up?" now answer, "Famous." Not fireman. Not president. Not mommy or daddy or teacher or cowboy. Famous. Our children want to be an adjective?

There is an e-mail going around (and around and around) that asks the reader to name the last five Heisman trophy winners, the last five Oscar winners, the last five Pulitzer Prize winners. Only the nerdiest of trivia nerds would be able to get all the answers, of course, and the punch line comes with the last questions: "Who was your first grade teacher? Who taught you to drive a car? Who gave you your first kiss?"

Thinly disguised moral of the story: Being famous doesn't equate with making a difference in the life of another human being.

I have to admit that, as I approached the masterpiece spiderweb, I half-expected to see something written in its strands, half-expected to find in its elegant tendrils a personal note, an answer to the deep heart question that had been keeping me company for weeks. I wanted to believe that Charlotte, not just a great writer but a great friend, had found her way to Sandhill.

But there was no message. At least not a visible one. There was no pronouncement of my terrific-ness or radiance or humility. No words proclaiming that I am "some woman." No answer to my question.

And yet, there in the morning sunlight, kneeling silently before that web, the lifework of an anonymous spider, I did get a message: a reminder that one life lived, one effort made, one web spun with passion and love, can change the world.

AUGUST 3, 2008

July in Georgia is not a pleasant month. Heat that chokes, insects that madden, and the unavoidable sensation of time passing as the garden begins to fade can leave even the most sanguine of us short-tempered and longing for the respite of shorter days and drier air.

It is a truth of some wide acceptance that July's only saving grace is tomatoes, home-grown and thick-sliced and dusted with a heavy shower of salt, fanned out on the plate beside fresh corn and fried okra or slathered with mayonnaise and slapped between two slices of white bread.

It is a truth of some wide acceptance but it is not tomatoes that refresh my heat-withered spirits, not the juvenile pleasure of juice dripping off my chin, not the eye-closing satisfaction of the warm taste of summer spreading through my mouth.

The sensation that pulls me back from the abyss of believing that I will never be cool again is the sight of a peanut field.

Unlike the cornstalks that stretch up into the sky, demanding their personal space while blocking the horizon, peanut vines grow close to the ground and spread into each others' arms, meshing their tender leaves and spindly stems into communal productivity.

Daddy, like the good farmer he is, rotates the location of his peanut fields, but every year, somewhere within sight of Sandhill's front porch, I can watch a field go from a graph of shallow gray ditches to a connect-the-dots game board of green pinpricks and, as the sunshine and water—God willing—come down in the right proportions, the dots get connected into endless straight lines that roll out like unspooled ribbon.

The spring before the summer that Sandhill was built, just before planting time, Daddy asked me, "You gonna build that house or not? It's time to plant peanuts." And when I couldn't give him a ground-breaking date, he plowed right across the three acres that had been marked with bright pink flags.

By July 2, the day the contractor and his helpers arrived to dig the footings, there were tiny little nuts, what Mama calls poppers, dangling from the vines they displaced. For the four months it took to build the house, the peanuts kept growing in what would be the front yard and the carpenters, the painters, the roofers all had the pleasure of pulling up a hill every now and then.

It's been seventeen years since that summer. Lots of things, of course, have changed. There's a deck hanging off the back of Sandhill. There are shrubs and trees planted where the peanut vines were. The two towheaded children who climbed all over the lumber stacked in the yard and picked up errant nails are grown. The dog who moved in with me is buried in the side yard.

And I've changed, too. But not just in the obvious, age-related ways. I've learned that farmers aren't the only ones who need to rotate their crops, that planting time can't be delayed, that the hottest, gnattiest moments will be survived.

In just a few weeks the multi-stepped process of harvest will begin; the plows first, then the pickers and trailers lumbering like the mechanical monsters in a science fiction movie. The sounds of their engines will fill the air as long as there is light and in a matter of days the fields will be flat and gray. I will have gotten my wish for shorter days and drier, cooler air.

For now, though, I sit on the front porch in a rocking chair in need of a fresh paint job, knees pulled up to my chest and bare feet hanging over the edge of the seat, and stare across the way at the mounded green lines, drawn toward the far edge of the field, the place where all the lines converge.

AUGUST 17, 2008

At 33,000 feet, levitating between earth and sky on a pallet of white clouds, I am neither here nor there. With no watch and with the cell phone turned off, I don't know the time. All the faces are the faces of strangers.

Flying always produces in me, contrary to what I would have imagined before ever taking my first plane trip, a meditative state. What is done is done. What is behind is behind. My usual tendency to reexamine, rehash, relive gets checked at the gate and, if I'm lucky, lost somewhere in the airport.

At 33,000 feet it is all anticipation.

But the plane can't stay suspended in the ether forever. Eventually it has to land. It must begin the slow, angled drop that will deposit me onto tarmac, into time. And with the descent comes the pain.

I understand the physiology: unequal pressure between the middle ear and the cabin of the airplane, pressure that can't be equalized as it normally would be by the Eustachian tube because the tube is blocked. And since the airflow is blocked the eardrum gets stretched; with the stretching comes the pain.

The only thing that makes it bearable is the knowledge that it won't last forever and that what awaits me on the ground is worth it.

Today, as I feel the pressure building, transforming itself from annoyance to discomfort to measurable pain, what awaits me on the ground are cooler temperatures and the hugs of two towheads. Not a bad trade-off. So I move my jaw up and down and back and forth, pump my finger in and out of my ear like a mascara wand, close my eyes, and visualize eighty-two degrees and a light wind.

And I find myself considering how often I have done just that in a less literal, more emotional way. How often I've been flying high, oblivious to everything not in Seat 27D, responsible for nothing beyond keeping my seat belt fastened when I gradually became aware of a growing buzz, something not exactly a noise, clearly not a voice, but definitely a sound rising in my ears. Aware, but not bothered.

How the buzzing got louder and interfered with my self-centered thoughts, got louder still and started pushing those thoughts out with something like a dull ache that grew into a sting into a throb, ignorable no longer. How most of the time, at just about the moment I thought I'd rather cut off that ear than hear what was being whispered into it, my plane touched safely down and rolled to a stop. And how, just as I was dragging my suitcase off the carousel at baggage claim, the words came, in clear translation and with the impact of a left hook, to show me the way to the parking lot and beyond.

The intercom crackles and breaks my train of thought. "We have been cleared to land," says the man in the navy blue suit behind the metal door. "Please return your seats to an upright position," instructs the flight attendant. I look out the tiny window; the clouds have disappeared and I can see buildings and highways and green.

Forrest Gump thought life was like a box of chocolates. Poets have offered that life is like a river, a coin, a journey, a battle, a puzzle. Today I'm thinking that life is a lot like a plane ride from Savannah to Baltimore with a layover in Atlanta. And I'm thinking that what I got for my money was more than biscotti cookies and "Thank you for flying Delta."

AUGUST 31, 2008

Life is not The Container Store.

Neither is Life my attic.

The Container Store is open and bright. Its aisles are wide and its shopping carts are shiny stainless steel.

The Container Store is filled with empty things (boxes, cabinets, trays, bottles) made from various materials (paper, glass, plastic, straw) offered for purchase by consumers who have items (socks, CDs, spices, staples) they wish to contain. The empty things are stacked and sorted on rows and rows of identical shelves set out on a grid that looks like a vast magnification of the graph paper we used in high school to plot coordinates for Miss Kemp.

The empty things are clean and clear. The empty things are beautiful and seductive. The empty things whisper, "I will make your life better if you will only take me home."

My attic looks nothing like The Container Store. It also has boxes, but none of them are empty. Some are labeled, some are not. A few match, most don't. All are gathering dust.

One box is all that is left of Ginny—her collar, her blanket, her vet records. For eleven years she came when I called, loved me when I didn't deserve loving, offered her ears as handkerchiefs. Another box is Wesleyan—birthday cards, programs, costumes, purple everything, reminders of the four years during which I figured out who I could be. There is one box that holds toys and puzzles from Adam's and Kate's childhoods, one that holds my Girl Scout badge and ceramic projects from summer camp, and a couple that hold secrets.

My attic is dark and, this time of year, hot. Some of the boxes are held together by packing tape. Some of them have been infiltrated by mice. All of them are surrounded by a great swathe of itchy insulation and a maze of PVC pipe.

The room at the top of the stairs would seem to have little resemblance to the pristine, almost Aryan, perfection of The Container Store. It would seem to be, in fact, at the opposite end of the spectrum.

I heard a song not long ago that began, "My yesterdays are all boxed up and neatly put away." The first time I heard it, I whispered to myself, "Yes!" The trapdoor to my mind's attic was closed and I smiled at the thought that I could walk down the hall under the swinging white cord with nary a notice. I had finally learned how to remember without recriminating, how to recall without reliving, how to recollect without rewriting.

What I hadn't learned, however, is that life, with all its unflagging determination to astonish, its frustrating lack of predictability and its constant requirement for recalibration, refuses to be contained. I hadn't learned that light bends. That the opposite ends of the spectrum—the spots where The Container Store, with its fresh and unused bins, and my attic, with its bruised and bulging boxes, lie—are, with all the flexing and twisting and turning, the same place.

You can get there by holding on to everything—every photo, every calendar, every ticket stub, or you can get there by holding on to nothing, turning your pockets inside out and opening your clenched fists. But you're still going to get there, the place where you finally figure out that, no matter how hard you try, life can't be controlled.

I hadn't learned it then, the day I heard that song for the first time, but I have now. And when I listen these days, I think I hear a little irony in Sheryl Crow's voice. I think she's learned it, too. That yesterday can't be boxed up. That it is never neatly put away. That life is not The Container Store and life is nobody's attic.

SEPTEMBER 14, 2008

Pedestrians have the right-of-way. The ones we get in the country, however, don't always cross at the corner or wait for the light.

When every trip begins on a dirt road you develop the ability, not quite an instinct, to respond to the sudden dart, the unexpected flash of fur that moves from periphery to focus in a fraction of a second. You learn that a rabbit generally runs straight across and the only effort needed to avoid it is a slight turn in the direction from which it came. You learn that a squirrel is decidedly undecided and the only thing you can do is grip the steering wheel, mutter "Please, please, please! Don't, don't, don't!" and hope you won't feel that slight thud under the chassis.

You wait for the wild turkey to stumble toward the ditch and, at the last possible moment, throw itself into the air. Deer, dashing across a field or out of the brush, call for nothing more than quick reflexes. Sometimes even that doesn't help. A turtle you just go around.

Rabbits, squirrels, turtles, deer. You get used to them.

This morning, however, there was something else. A pedestrian I'd never encountered before. A sudden flash at the corner of my eye and then, headed straight into the path of the car, something long and wet, fat and round. In that strange way that the human brain processes thousands of pieces of information in less than a second, I experienced simultaneously panic and repulsion and fear, exactly what anyone experiences when The Unknown takes material shape and invades one's conscious.

As I lifted my foot from the accelerator and goose bumps rose on my arms, I realized that the creature was a beaver, not yet full grown, his dark wet fur plastered against his skin and glistening in the morning sunshine. He had darted from the pond that comes right up to the edge of the pavement straight onto the county-maintained road and, clearly, had no idea that his impulsivity would land him in harm's way.

Spinning around on himself, he scurried back the way he had come and disappeared over the edge of the dam. I shook myself to dispel the goose bumps and sped back up.

This has been the summer of the funerals. Eight since the first of June. I am weary of funerals. Weary of watching the faces of people I love reflecting the pain of losses that cannot be recouped. Weary of trying to find words that do not sound trite and insincere. Weary, quite frankly, of the flowers and food and fatigue of jarringly inane conversation.

It is not as though death is a stranger. It is, as the paradoxical cliché tells us, a part of life. But no one, not even the most exhausted caregiver, is ever prepared.

Most of the deaths I've noted this summer were like the rabbit or squirrel or even the deer: I was startled out of my ordinary daily routine but responded appropriately without thinking. Three times it was the long-ill mother of a friend. Twice a grandparent of someone close.

A couple, though, were like that unfamiliar, chill-producing beaver. Out of place, stunning. They left me reminded in jarring terms that all we hold close, all that motivates us to get up each morning, all that provides any meaning is so ephemeral, so transient, so temporary.

They reminded me that despite our ridiculous efforts at preparedness—whether for a hurricane that never arrives or the death of someone we love—, life is a series of shocks and surprises. Some are heartbreaking, some are delights. Some are history-altering, some are inconsequential to all but a few. Some are nothing more than inconveniences, all are pedestrians demanding the right-of-way. And as for all pedestrians, the only thing to do is slow down and watch what happens.

SEPTEMBER 28, 2008

So, a tree falls in the woods or, in this particular situation, across a dirt road. Whether it made a sound is somewhat irrelevant when the road across which it has fallen is the road to one's house. Silent or cacophonous, the result of the arboreal capitulation is the same—impeded access.

We have had quite a few downed trees in our corner of the county this year. Several have fallen on power lines, leaving us waiting perhaps not so patiently while the folks from Excelsior Electric made their way slowly through arteries to arterioles to capillaries. Most of them, however, have landed, without any interference, to very neatly bisect the road and divide the world into those at home and those away.

The unusual number of collapses is due, I think, to several reasons. The heavy equipment of loggers who have been harvesting the forests along the road have weakened the trees' root systems. County road maintenance includes dragging the ditches for debris, a practice that results in the trees closest to the road balancing on smaller and smaller pedestals. And, of course, some of the trees are just old. They hit the ground and, instead of splintering, dissolve into the finest of sawdust.

Whatever the reason, we've all learned to be watchful this summer, to pay closer attention to what lies ahead in the rocky gray dust.

At least I thought I had.

Driving home the other afternoon, not just daydreaming but completely lost in somber contemplation, I topped the hill and was jolted back into reality by the sight of a tree stretched across the road as though it had simply gotten tired and decided to lie down. It was a scrub oak, gray and gnarly, bare of any foliage, its branches thin and bent at odd sharp angles. It covered about three quarters of the road, leaving just enough room on the far side to ease a car by without sliding into the ditch.

Having hit the brakes at first sight, I maneuvered the car slowly between the topmost branches and the slanted face of the ditch with inches to spare on either side. I drove the remaining half-mile to home and promptly forgot about the tree.

Until the next morning when it startled me coming from the other direction. And then that afternoon when it surprised me again. After a couple of days it occurred to me that no one was going to move the tree.

The tree was not a sapling. It could not be dragged out of the road by one or even two people. It would have to be cut up or pulled away by a tractor pulling a heavy chain. I, having neither a chainsaw nor a tractor, had no responsibility for the removal. But because I traveled that way every day, I had to be aware of its presence, had to circumnavigate its substantial self, had to avoid the dangers that it offered simply by being.

After about a week of making a loop around the poor dead tree twice a day, it occurred to me that I was probably supposed to be learning something, something beyond the idea that it would be handy to have my own chainsaw. Something along the lines of: There are things in life over which I have no control, whether minor annoyances or life-changing events, and if I'm going to be able to keep moving, not be wrecked on the rocks or stuck on the sandbar, I can't just wait for someone else to come along and remove the obstacle. I, on my own and for myself, have to find a way around.

I have to be honest. That doesn't necessarily appeal to me. Not the thought of having to find my own way. I'm really good at that. No, the part that makes my fur stand up is the necessity of acknowledging that my own way will sometimes have to be around, not through. That more often than not I'll be hugging the edge of the ditch rather than straddling the centerline. And that getting home will take more effort than I thought.

In that case, it would then seem fairly obvious, that whatever it is one is trying to get to had better be worth the trouble.

OCTOBER 12, 2008

You wake up one morning. You walk outside. You take a breath and you know. There is a peanut field somewhere that has been turned over, the peanuts thrown onto their backs and left to dry as they wait for the harvest.

You know this because of the scent: damp earth and nitrogen. It is the perfume of a South Georgia October. It hovers over the yards and roads, seeps into the houses and alerts those who sleep in those houses to be aware of slow-moving vehicles grunting their way toward town hauling jewels weighed by the ton, not the carat. The languor of late summer has shifted into the urgency of harvest.

And while there is no canonized text or organized presbytery, this work, this repetition, this ritual is as much liturgy as is holy communion. Those who plant and plow and pray for rain are the priests who tend the temple of the earth year after year, who keep the fires lit and offer the sacrifices of hard labor and harder faith on behalf of the rest of us.

I was not born with dirt under my fingernails. I came late to the life of farming, a recalcitrant teenaged companion to my father's following his bliss. I resented the dust and the isolation of the dirt road. I came as close as I ever have to cursing as I ran barefoot across a field in blistering heat helping chase a blind cow. I couldn't wait to be gone.

I left for college before the first harvest. It was seven years before I returned. By that time I had, mercifully, learned a few things and that fall, standing on the front porch as my father and my brother, covered in dust and bone-weary, climbed into the cabs of their trucks and jerked their way up that dirt road pulling trailers into the quickly waning light, I bowed my head and prayed.

Prayed for the daylight to last so that the trailers could be seen by other vehicles, prayed that the tires would hold up, prayed for all the traffic lights going through town to be green. Prayed for every farmer in every truck pulling every trailer in every town.

That was twenty-seven years ago. The highway into town is four-laned all the way now so the people with tags from Gwinnett and Cobb and Fulton don't get to blow their horns and shake their fists quite as much anymore, but not much else has changed.

There's still a chance that the rain won't come soon enough to loosen the ground and the peanuts will fall off the vine as they are plowed up. Or that, once they're plowed up and drying, the rain will come and produce mold. It's quite likely that a fully-loaded trailer will blow a tire at some point.

But what's certain is that the hum of the plows and the pickers will begin with daylight and continue long after sunset. That the men driving them will pause only long enough to disengage a knot of vines from the plow and swig down a Coke or a jar of iced tea. That the last load will be the subject of great rejoicing. That the earth will yield its increase and be gladly put to bed.

You wake up one morning. You walk outside. You take a breath and you know. There is a peanut field somewhere that has been turned over and the call to worship has been sung. Hallelujah. Hallelujah. Amen.

OCTOBER 26, 2008

It started about three weeks ago. Tap. Tap. Tap. Silence for about thirty seconds, then tap. Tap. Tap.

I walked to the door and saw a mockingbird dive-bombing the patio door. Beak against glass. Tap. Tap. Tap.

Poor thing, I thought. He sees his reflection in the glass and wants to scare away that other bird. And I got all thoughtful, saw myself in the mockingbird—that way that I tend to notice, analyze, and criticize in others the things in myself that most make me want to cringe.

Poor thing.

But then I walked outside onto the deck. Sympathy and thoughtfulness evaporated. All over the deck railings, the deck floor, and the lawn chair were bird droppings. Purple and white poop interspersed with unidentified seeds.

I forgot about self-analysis and insight. I forgot about appreciation of the natural world. I forgot about life lessons. I was nothing less than completely irritated.

No more "Poor thing." Now it was "Come on, stupid bird. How many times do you have to crash your brain into the glass before you figure it out? And why in the world do you have to poop every time you do it?" I'm sure there is an actual answer to that last question, but I'm not sure I want to know it.

I sighed—not a shallow, slightly sad exhalation, but a deep, forceful expulsion—and went back inside. At least, I reminded myself, someone was coming the next day to pressure wash the house. What fortunate timing.

The next morning Travis sprayed off a couple years' worth of dust and cobwebs and dirt dauber nests and kamikaze mockingbird poop. The deck railings, along with the front porch rockers which had also been victimized, were sparkling white. I stood with my hands on my hips breathing in the early autumn air and lapsed back into generosity toward the poor bird.

Travis hadn't been gone for fifteen minutes when I heard it. Tap. Tap. Tap.

No! Not again!

Yes. Again. Bright purple splotches at the foot of the patio door, along the railings.

If I were a woman bent toward profanity I would probably have uttered some at that moment. Instead all I could muster was, like Charlie Brown, a long loud drawn-out, "AAUUGGHH!!"

A handful of wet wipes later, most of the avian fecal matter had been cleaned up. An hour later the whole process (Tap. Tap. Tap. AAUUGGHH!! Wipe.) was repeated when I discovered that the bird had resumed his attack on the front porch windows.

By sundown I had given up. Thrown in the wet wipes. Raised the wing of the mockingbird and declared him the undisputed champ.

It's been three weeks. The splotches have multiplied and dried into powdery Rorschach tests. New ones greet me every afternoon. The tapping continues and I find myself wondering if, like the anonymous narrator of "The Raven," I should just open the door and invite the bird in. Maybe he has something to say.

And, of course, he does. It is, in fact, exactly what I heard him saying before I got so angry and stopped listening. It is always myself that I see in the intolerant, ungrateful, and indecisive. It is my hands that remain folded in the presence of so much need, my voice that remains silent in a world that needs to hear truth.

Are you ... tap ... going to keep doing ... tap, tap, tap ... the same old things ... tap, tap, tap ... and expect different results ... tap, tap ... or are you ... tap ... going to ... tap, tap, tap ... stop the madness ... tap, tap, tap ... and fly?

NOVEMBER 9, 2008

The autumn dusk was just beginning to fall. There was the slightest suggestion of a chill in the air. The campus of the big city church was, for the most part, still and quiet.

Just across a small courtyard from the solid sanctuary with its flagstone narthex and exposed buttresses was the prayer chapel. Made of the same stone as the church, its six walls enclosed an area hardly bigger than a master bedroom. The circular altar, made from a three-hundred-pound piece of Jerusalem stone, had one of the Hebrew names for God carved on each of its four sides. It was centered beneath a suspended cross and surrounded by a kneeling bench of iron wrought to resemble a crown of thorns. The ceiling above the cross extended up two stories and ended with a skylight.

I looked over at my friend Margaret. She had known I would love this place. "Would you like a few minutes?" she asked and then quietly slipped out the heavy wooden doors, leaving me alone.

I stood at the altar, tilting my head back as far as it would go to look through the skylight at the quickly fading day, took a deep breath, and lowered myself down onto the kneeler.

I was tired. And sick. And anxious. If anybody needed to be kneeling in a quiet place and opening her heart to healing it was I.

And oh, yes, I was grieving, too. Grieving over the death of my friend, the one who in the darkest time of my life always ended our telephone conversations with, "I'll say a rosary for you tonight." It was a soothing image even to this non-Catholic, the image of someone moving her fingers over worn beads, repeating sacred words, and calling my name.

I folded my hands tightly together like a child playing "Here's The Church," felt my chin fall to my chest, and heard myself praying.

I don't know what I prayed, just that words came out and drifted up and got caught in the great whirlwind of breath that constantly rises to worship that which is not—and never will be—human. I felt my eyelashes grow heavy with tears that did not fall, but floated, trembling like an over-full cup.

This wasn't my place. I had no history here. Had not witnessed baptisms or weddings or taken communion at this altar. Had not sung hymns or recited creeds under this roof or watched sunlight shoot through these stained glass windows to draw hopscotch courses on the floor. And yet it became in those moments a sacred place. One of my sacred places.

I have quite a few of them. Since I know that the sacred cannot be contained within the walls of any one church or even all the churches put together, that the sacred cannot be contained at all, I have learned to find it everywhere.

The Celtic cross in the middle of Wesley Memorial Garden on St. Simons, surrounded by the unruly flowers and shrubs of the coast, is a sacred place. So is the top of the Temple Mound at the Ocmulgee National Monument, the ground around a particular fire-scorched pine tree just inside the property line behind Mama and Daddy's house, and the rooftop deck on a certain beach house.

They are all places where I have experienced grace, the unexpected outpouring of the weighty yet ephemeral assurance that, as Julian of Norwich said, all shall be well and all shall be well and all manner of things shall be well.

I blinked and the over-full cup emptied on my cheeks. A self-baptism, as it were.

I stood and walked toward the door where I noticed a set of votive candles on either side, a very non-Protestant accoutrement to worship. I felt the skin around my mouth loosen as the corners rose into a smile.

Okay, Nancy, I thought as I picked up the lighter, this one is for you.

The wick flickered and then caught, stretching itself into the air, into my breath, into grace.

NOVEMBER 23, 2008

Grandmama was a gardener. The kind who wandered around in the woods digging up anything that looked interesting and taking it home to root. The kind who sent people away clutching damp paper towels wrapped around something spindly with the promise that it would most definitely absolutely grow. The kind who thought the house could take care of itself and that the best place to be, regardless of how hot or cold, was outside.

Her yard was a quilt of flower beds and brick-edged paths. Outside the back door was a patch of succulents that seemed to multiply like science fiction clones and flanking the front door were two cedar trees she nursed from saplings so that by the time I was a teenager they were tall enough to decorate with fat, colored Christmas lights.

Fig trees and hydrangeas. Mimosa trees and Cherokee roses. Petunias and verbena. Wisteria and honeysuckle. Grandmama's green thumb touched them all.

I'm really not much of a gardener. I tend to forget to water things that need watering and to prune things that need pruning. The pollen of practically everything that grows within two miles of Sandhill makes my eyes red, my nose run, and my head ache. So instead of getting my hands down into the dirt, etching my cuticles with the deep chocolate of potting soil, I have generally depended upon the pity of my parents or the pecuniary interest of professionals.

Until recently. Until this spring when, at the behest of a plant-loving friend, I planted some rosemary and lavender and, over the next few months, watched the seeds break the soil in thin green sprigs and then straighten themselves into tall slender stalks.

One afternoon I rubbed a few leaves between my fingers— rosemary in one hand, lavender in the other—and carried the two scents with me for the rest of the day.

Then a couple of weeks ago I found myself with one foot in a ditch, the other braced against the bank on the other side, trying to dig up an American beautyberry bush. I was there because my friend Debra had told me, along with our friend Emily, that the large beautyberry bush in her backyard had been rooted from a tiny one she had found in the woods.

Being the kind of women to whom such a remark becomes an immediate challenge, Emily and I soon found ourselves armed with two shovels and more enthusiasm than sense as we drove slowly down the dirt road leading to Sandhill, scouting the ditches for the bright flare of color that would pinpoint our targets: spindly little roadside trees whose neon-magenta berries appear along with the first cool snap and just about the time the chartreuse leaves begin dropping.

There was one near a tree stump! Another one at the foot of a scrub oak!

But these were not baby bushes like the ones Debra had found; these were two and three feet high and just as wide and one quick jab of the shovel into the sandy dirt around the first demonstrated that beauty berry bushes are blessed with very well-developed root systems. The digging radius got wider and wider, deeper and deeper.

Just when I was about to suggest that we abort the mission, one more massive tug dislodged the bush from the dirt and sent me stumbling backwards and trying not to end up on my backside at the bottom of the bank. An equally emphatic pull by Emily and we stood in the middle of the road, holding up our bushes like weekend fishermen showing off the big catch.

Twenty minutes later I'd sent Emily back in the direction of Gwinnett County and stuck my beauty berry in a bucket of water to await planting.

And, suddenly, it seemed as though Grandmama was there, standing under the carport with me, staring at bush's hairy roots waving in the water, asking me where I thought I'd plant it, telling me where she thought it might do well.

I doubt that a rose bed or cutting garden ever finds a place at Sandhill. Or that trellises and pergolas draped with Confederate jasmine or honeysuckle ever guard the driveway. But I'm encouraged that the sycamore tree in the backyard seems to have established itself and the gardenia under the kitchen window is still alive. And as soon as I get a few minutes, that beautyberry bush is going into the ground.

DECEMBER 7, 2008

This time of year, between about seven-thirty and eight in the morning, there is a moment when, coming around the big curve on Adabelle Road, you get blinded by the sunlight. Blinded by a flash so brilliant that it takes your breath away.

And in that moment, that half-second of total lack of vision, there is absolutely nothing to do but trust—trust your muscle memory from thirty-five years of navigating that same curve and trust any oncoming drivers to stay on their side of the road.

It's a scary thing, trust.

One bright summer Sunday Jason finally made good on his promise to take me out on his sailboat, a little Hobie. We pushed off from East Beach on St. Simons into the cool turquoise water and Jason began maneuvering the ropes and sails in short, quick movements while I sat idly on the tight canvas.

I had my back to the ocean, watching the bright dots of people stretched out along the beach. I could feel the shallow waves bumping underneath us as we moved away from shore.

We'd gotten no farther than the sandbar when I felt the boat rise suddenly on a building wave. "Hold on!" Jason screamed and I reached out to grab, I think, the mast as the rear of the boat rose straight into the air.

"Let go!" he screamed almost immediately and I opened my fists as I felt myself being thrown into the water headfirst.

I came up gasping, looking around for the boat and for Jason. The wave that had catapulted the boat head over heels was long gone, spread smoothly out onto the beach like cake icing.

We managed to wrestle the boat back upright and, still trying to catch our breaths, paddled back to shore while Jason explained that had I not let go, had I not responded to his command without thought, I would have taken a blow to my head with the boom, a blow that—most likely—would have left me unconscious and, quite possibly, drowned.

All very dramatic.

Only later, after we'd told the story three or four times—with appropriate embellishment, of course—to the folks on the beach who'd been able to do nothing except watch as the little Hobie "turtled" and threw us into the air, did I fully understand the extent of the danger we'd encountered only a few yards from shore and in chest-high water.

Just a few days ago, in the midst of a conversation that I'd not really wanted to have, the person to whom I was talking responded to my long, drawn-out, far-more-intense-than-I'd-intended diatribe with two softly-spoken words: Trust me.

I didn't know at that moment whether I could or not. Didn't know if I even wanted to. And I remembered, for what at the time seemed no reason at all, that day on the Hobie. That day when, in response to "Hold on!" and "Let go!" (Interestingly enough, also two words.), I had done exactly as I was told without having any idea why.

I didn't have time to think about whether it was a good idea. Didn't know enough about sailing to determine on my own whether I stood a better chance one way or the other. I just knew Jason.

That's all trust is, really. Acting in response to what you know about the person, not the situation. It's what throws a baby off the counter into her father's arms. It's what sends the underdog back onto the field from the coach's huddle. It's what threw me off that sailboat and into the ocean. The father, the coach, the friend.

Trust me, the voice on the telephone repeated. And I found myself answering, I do.

DECEMBER 21, 2008

In December there's usually not a lot of daylight left over Sandhill when I get home, but last Friday I got there earlier than usual and was able to see the rather pitiful state into which the backyard had fallen.

There was a lone and empty hummingbird feeder dangling from one shepherd's crook and an overgrown hanging basket of mint from another. The dandelions that I had so energetically pulled up by the roots and left to dry in the unseasonable warmth the previous weekend had become piles of slimy green mush in the week's rain. It was all a stark and embarrassing contrast to the bright and festive inside where the tree stood so humbly regal in the corner of the living room and candles stood like posted guards on all the tabletops.

I'd gotten most of the dead mint stems plucked and had started on the dandelion piles when I got the oddest sensation that someone had just tapped me on the shoulder. I stood up quickly and turned to see a what looked like a huge egg yolk rising slowly, as on a hydraulic lift of some kind, over the horizon.

With the perspective of a couple hundred yards the bright yellow bulb seemed to stretch the full depth of the tree line that marks the edge of the farm. It felt almost as though the rising had a pulse, that the gravitational pull that creates the tides was reaching far inland to draw me farther out into the wake.

I've been a full-moon watcher for years now. Each one makes me melancholy for all the ones I missed before I started acknowledging the wonder and I am always enraptured by the liquid silver light that spills out over the landscape.

But this one was different.

This full moon, at the end of the year just before Christmas, had something to say, and in order to make itself heard over the din it had come nearly 19,000 miles closer than usual. When something, or somebody, goes to that much trouble to get my attention I tend to drop what I'm doing and listen.

So I stopped. Got still. Took a deep breath. Listened to the moon.

Funny thing: The voice I heard was remarkably like my own and the words were familiar ones. "You know all you need to know."

For someone whose college major focused on popular culture and current events, I am remarkably uninformed these days. I don't watch CNN or Fox News. I don't have a Blackberry and learned to text only because it is my niece Kate's preferred form of communication. I have two friends who save their *People* magazines for me so that when I visit for the weekend I can at least familiarize myself with what passes for celebrity these days and not go out in public sounding foolish by asking questions like "Who is Lindsay Lohan?"

But I know all I need to know.

I know that truth will always win out. I know that patience, especially the kind that is tinged with pain, is both the result of and the source of strength. I know that the only real power I have is the power to choose.

I know that the dearest and deepest attachments are the ones that cannot be explained. I know that silence is a language too few people speak. And I know that Christmas, like the moon, has a message.

And all we have to do is listen.

JANUARY 1, 2009

It was quite by accident that I discovered that an extra second was going to be added to 2008. A "leap second" it was called, an addition to atomic clocks that meant that the very last minute of 2008 actually contained sixty-one seconds.

First they tell me Pluto isn't really a planet and now I have to get my arms around a sixty-one-second minute?

According to the folks at CNN, the world's official clock (the Coordinated Universal Time), which is used for broadcasting time signals and is essential for running GPS and the Internet, is "extremely accurate." "By comparison," they go on to say, "the Earth is far less reliable."

There's something about that statement that raises my cockles. Who is CNN, or anyone else for that matter, to call the Earth unreliable? Doesn't the sun come up every morning? Don't the seasons move in and out of the world's revolving door in a relatively orderly fashion? Doesn't the tide push and pull dependably enough that sailors managed to circumnavigate the globe long before GPS?

I am not a Luddite. I write these words on a computer. I lock and unlock my car by remote access, as they say. I have grown increasingly attached to my cracker-sized iPod. But it bothers me that we, all of us, have become so dependent upon precision.

Airlines schedule flights to leave at 10:43 and passengers start hyperventilating when, at 10:45, the plane is still awaiting clearance to take off.

At the Beijing Olympics, Usain Bolt won the gold medal and set the world record in the men's 100-meter dash, finishing in 9.69 seconds. The silver medalist finished two-tenths of a second slower and no one outside the track and field community remembers his name.

A couple of nights ago, when the moon was the thinnest sliver of silver light dangling over the flat and empty acres of the farm, I stopped what I was doing to stare at the stars. They looked like a handful of diamonds strewn carelessly across a black velvet scarf. There was just enough chill in the air to make me pull my arms tight to my chest as I stretched my neck to take it all in.

I don't know how long I stood there. The clarity I breathed in, the hope that settled on my shoulders, the smile that raised itself like a flag cannot be measured in time.

A new year is always an unsettling combination of anticipation and anxiety—this one, perhaps, more than any in my recent memory. In the world delineated by political boundaries and in the one delineated by my random thoughts, there are questions whose answers exist but are not yet visible. There are choices whose consequences are not yet manifest. There are opportunities whose rewards are not yet imagined. And neither the questions nor the choices nor the opportunities will be resolved in one extra second.

The people at CNN say that the unreliability of the Earth is based upon its inability to rotate at a constant speed, its tendency to wobble as a result of volcanoes and earthquakes and such. That makes our planet sound a lot like each of us, subject to our own volcanoes and earthquakes.

What doesn't sound like us, with our calendar-turning uncertainties, is the idea that by adding a leap second every now and then we can make sure that "the Sun remains overhead at noon."

I'm not ready for that responsibility. Any extra seconds that I am offered will be spent watching the stars and wishing on any that happen to fall.

JANUARY 18, 2009

Aunt Rozzie died. Mama told me this morning. The visitation is tonight. I will drive to Cobbtown and I will see lots of relatives. I will see some people I don't know. I will see some people who are in both groups.

We will stand around and talk. We will fill the funeral home air with reminiscences and stories and exclamations on how much or how little we have all changed since the last time we saw each other.

Some of us, Mama included, will make a point of surveilling the flowers and potted plants, reading the cards pinned to wide pastel ribbons, and cooing blessings over the kind souls who sent them.

Back at my cousin Vera's house there will be Pyrex dishes of squash casserole and macaroni and cheese. There will be cakes— most of them these days, sadly enough, bought at the Walmart deli instead of baked in somebody's oven. The fried chicken will have, most likely, come from the same place, but the sweet tea will be home-brewed.

I know all these things because one does not grow up Southern without learning them, without absorbing and being branded by them.

I can remember sitting in the car as a young child outside Barnes Mortuary in the late evening of a sultry summer, watching men and women move in quiet waves up the steps and across the porch into rooms lit with yellow light. There was a small group of men on the lawn smoking, the tips of their cigarettes hovering like lightning bugs in front of their faces. They all wore suits and white shirts and lace-up shoes.

The car windows were rolled down and I could hear crickets and night birds and the whooshing of other cars going by on Savannah Avenue. Keith and I played silly games, made up songs, tried to recognize the faces moving up the dark sidewalk.

Sometime later, Mama, wearing one of her Sunday dresses, and Daddy, dressed just like the men on the lawn, would reappear, pause on the steps to speak to one or two people, and return to us, exactly the same as when they had left. Looking at death, speaking of death had not changed them.

I would understand later, much later, how wrong I was.

I don't get to sit in the car these days. I'm grown—or as grown as I'll ever be—and I am a part of the quiet wave that moves in and out. I take the pen chained to the lectern and sign my own name to the book. I stand in line to shake the hands or hug the necks of the family and stumble over such simple words: I'm sorry.

Last week I took a field trip to the bookstore. I wandered around a while and found myself in the poetry section where I saw, front facing out, *Selected Poems* by John Donne. A friend had mentioned Donne in conversation the week before and so I took it as a sign that I needed to revisit the poet I'd not read in probably thirty years.

The last selection in the book is Donne's famous "Meditation XVII," best known as the source of the title of a Hemingway novel and which includes these lines:

"All mankind is of one author, and is one volume; when one man dies, one chapter is not torn out of the book, but translated into a better language; and every chapter must be so translated...As therefore the bell that rings to a sermon, calls not upon the preacher only, but upon the congregation to come: so this bell calls us all ... No man is an island, entire of itself...any man's death diminishes me, because I am involved in mankind; and therefore never send to know for whom the bell tolls; it tolls for thee."

Whether one believes in an afterlife of eternal youthfulness and an absence of pain or whether one believes that the last breath is simply the last breath, we engage in the ritual, we perform the rites as a reminder to listen for the bell.

FEBRUARY 1, 2009

On cold winter mornings, when the windows were etched with ice doilies, I got to lie in bed five more minutes as Daddy spun the thermostat and the deep-bellied sigh of the floor furnace came up through the floor.

On cold winter mornings, when the light outside was the clear navy blue of just-dawn, I left the bed and let the warm air of the furnace billow up my pajama legs and arms before I jumped into my Buster Brown turtleneck and plaid pleated skirt and knee socks.

On cold winter mornings, when the wind whistled around the corners of the house like a freight train, I got a grilled cheese sandwich for breakfast -- thick slices of bright orange hoop cheese melted onto soft white Sunbeam bread -- while Mama warmed my shoes on the open door of the oven.

On cold winter mornings, when the ground was hard and the ruts from the latest rain had stiffened into the fluted edge of a pie crust, Daddy went outside to warm up the car and came back in, rubbing his ungloved hands together, and stood patiently while we gathered our books and put on our coats.

On cold winter mornings, I first became conscious of the small, tender acts of love that parents perform for their children.

Children, of course, are oblivious. They have no awareness of the inequity of the relationship. And that is as it should be. Children have no means to do anything of significance for those who feed and clothe and house them. They are without any capacity for reciprocity.

Except, of course, that what is true in the literal food-clothing-shelter sense is completely false in all the ways that matter. Children, as anyone who has ever kissed the back of one's neck knows, offer back to the adults in their lives magic and wonder and laughter.

Children give us an excuse to read aloud and say words like "Today you are You, that is truer than true. There is no one alive who is Youer than You" and "He brought everything back, all the food for the feast. And he, he himself, the Grinch, carved the roast beast." They give us an excuse to do the Hokey-Pokey and ride the carousel and make construction-paper turkeys out of handprints.

Just after Christmas I took Aden, who is now six and in kindergarten, to see *The Tale of Despereaux*. Aden's sister Azlan and five other adults went with us, but it was really just about the two of us.

Aden knows about my fear of mice and all the stories of my encounters with the rodents (he has heard them so many times that he could probably tell them himself), so he understood what it took for me to voluntarily agree to sit and watch Despereaux (admittedly cute, admittedly animated, but still a mouse) and all his friends and family cavort on the big screen for an hour and a half.

As we got out of the cars and headed to the ticket office, Aden took my hand and said, "Aunt Kap, I think you are very brave."

Ah, yes. That is why we—the grown-ups, the authorities, the ones who convince ourselves that we are in control—do what we do. Get up early to turn up the heat, make grilled cheese sandwiches, read the same book over and over and over, watch movies about mice who talk. Work hard and sleep less than we should. Because if we are lucky, a very wise towhead with chocolate eyes will one day look up at us and say, "I think you are very brave."

FEBRUARY 15, 2009

When the county road crew drags the ditches of my dirt road, the two-mile drive from the paved road to Sandhill becomes an obstacle course. Roots and rocks make the surface of the road, usually relatively smooth and flat, look something like the pictures of the moon that the Apollo astronauts sent back to those of us staring up at the sky ooh-ing and ah-ing.

The result of this change in landscape, for the driving public, is that the shocks on whatever vehicle one is operating get a workout normally seen only in commercials shot in the Baja Peninsula. Tires bounce, steering wheels jerk, anything hanging from the rearview mirror sways like a pendulum on speed, and one cannot avoid thoughts of the yolks of a dozen eggs staining the carpet in the cargo area.

Last week was our week. Whatever rotation it is that the county maintains for ditch-dragging, a rotation that has to take into consideration weather conditions and the availability of correctional institute labor, resulted in our road getting itself torn up on Friday.

Driving home, happy for the weekend and thinking about my Saturday plans, I nonchalantly made the turn from pavement to red clay and suddenly felt my shoulders jolting against the seatbelt, my head making contact with the roof of the car. Ba-bump.

You can't drive fast on a road whose ditches have just been emptied of months of debris. You drive slowly and carefully, maneuvering left and right with the finesse of an ice sculptor, and you pay close attention to that around which you are maneuvering. Rocks and roots won't blow a tire, but a lost plow point will.

Most of the time I am slightly irritated by the care I have to exert on such days. Most of the time I mutter uncharitable things about the mounds of dirt and the people who left them there.

Most of the time I am not the least bit interested in why this inconvenience is regularly inflicted upon us dirt-road dwellers.

But Friday was different. Maybe just because I was happy for the weekend and thinking about my Saturday plans, I paid attention—to the extent that I could without driving straight into one of them—to the raw cuts in the walls of the ditches, the way the different colors of clay looked like a cutaway of the layers of the earth in my elementary school science book. I noticed how deep the ditches were, now emptied of branches and dead leaves. And I realized how easily would now flow the rainwaters that were sure to come with what General Beauregard Lee had just told us would be an early spring.

That's the thing about water: To be of any benefit, it has to flow. It can't be allowed to sit, to stay, to stagnate. And if its conduit—a ditch, an irrigation pipe, the spout of a watering can—is clogged with waste, that is exactly what happens.

So we drag the ditches, bore out the pipe, flush the spout, give water a channel through which it can run, through which it spreads out to nourish and clean.

I'm not always as prompt to do that as I should be. I get distracted, I let the dead leaves of unfinished tasks settle in the channel of my heart, I ignore the sludge of negative emotions that slows the stream of kindness. And, before I know it, the channel overflows and the road is washed out.

Stranded. Two miles from home.

The choice, then, isn't so hard. Drive carefully. Avoid the roots and rocks and, when the weather turns, let it rain.

MARCH 1, 2009

The honking startled me as I started out the back door. Over the field just east of the house, two Canada geese were gliding just a few feet above the ground. They were so close I could see the white chinstraps that made them look as though they were recovering from cosmetic surgery.

It was about 7:30, bright and chilly, and the geese were the only noise in the early morning landscape. They had risen from the pond and, in just a few moments, would head back that way, would settle down in the water side by side. For the moment, though, they were dancing—swooping and diving and curving in identical patterns, the kind I used to make in grade school by holding two pencils in one hand.

And they were singing to each other. Loud and nasal, the male's deep notes were instantly repeated by the female's slightly higher ones. The carport created an echo chamber that turned their song into a repeating refrain.

I stood there for a long time, unconcerned about the cold that was making my fingers stiff and mesmerized by their nearness, their naturalness, their nonchalance. All of it—the flying, the honking, the staying together—seemed so easy.

The next week I read that Geoffrey Chaucer, master of Middle English storytelling but not one generally known for his knowledge of ornithology, wrote that birds choose their mates on February 14. My geese had been frolicking just a couple days before Valentine's Day and I decided they must have been engaging in an early anniversary celebration.

I am accustomed to seeing flocks of geese slicing through the sky over Sandhill during the winter. At least once every year I find myself standing in the front yard with my neck bent back, hoping to see one of them break formation, leave a gap in the vee and veer off to find a life of nonconformity.

That, of course, is not going to happen. Canada geese, like most animals, are predictable, their habits certain, their conduct sure. They fly south in winter, back north in spring. They travel in groups. They mate for life.

Our culture doesn't value predictability and conformity very much. Entertainers, politicians, artists, all those in the public forum proclaim the value of being a maverick. Even athletes, whose very notoriety arises from an activity that requires a concerted effort by a number of people (something called a team), get more attention for individual behavior that is outrageous and shocking.

Having watched my geese for those few moments that morning, though, I figured out that it is the predictability, the certainty, the unvarying nature of their lives that draws our attention, that creates the beauty for those of us who watch. I realized that I don't really want one of them to break the symmetry of the vee.

It is comforting, when the stock market falls 600 points in one day, to know that the cardinals will still be hopping around the edges of the fields picking up seeds with their yellow beaks. It is reassuring, when the unemployment statistics are at their highest level in twenty years, to know that the daffodils will soon be breaking the skin of the earth and waving in the breeze. It is soothing, when the newspaper prints six pages of foreclosure notices, to watch two geese, sweethearts through and through, dance like nobody's watching.

MARCH 15, 2009

Like the first page of a toddler's sticker book—"This is a circle. This is yellow."—the moon is pasted dead center on a purple-black sky. Just the faintest trace of blue cheese veins creep across its face and the lemon light that spreads past its clean edge is pale and luminous, the only thing that suggests the circle might be three-dimensional.

A morning moon. Infinitesimally close to full. Teasing me into wishing the day away so that I can sit on the deck, the workday satisfactorily over, and breathe in the scent of almost-spring, marvel that the earth's personal satellite has made it all the way around one more time.

Morning moons, early tomatoes, three-year-olds who read. Not aberrations exactly, but phenomena just different enough to be phenomena, to elicit surprise and, then, wonder.

Rachel Carson, the marine biologist and writer who is credited with drawing the first serious attention to the environmental movement in the 1960s, said, "If I had influence with the good fairy who is supposed to preside over the christening of all children, I should ask that her gift to each child in the world be a sense of wonder so indestructible that it would last throughout life."

I have my doubts as to whether the good fairy was present to bestow that particular gift on me, but I do know that sense of wonder—the one that makes me pull over to the side of the road to watch a hawk try over and over to lift a rabbit from the apron of the highway, the one that lures me to lie on my back on one of the mounds at Ocmulgee and feel the rhythm of a passing train in my bones, the one that calls me out in the middle of the night to bathe my feet in the salt water of the sea—is mine and it has lasted. Lasted longer than childhood, longer than the years of trying too hard at everything, longer than my fruitless efforts at finding a cause for every effect.

That sense of wonder has had me dancing barefoot in the front yard under a chuppah of stars, burying my face in a slice of watermelon too big to hold, staring down a sunset that sets a lake on fire. It has made me braver and stronger and more content than anyone has a right to be.

I've been asked quite often of late from whence come the images that end up as words for other people to read and each time I am embarrassed that I cannot explain. I want to explain, but there is no explanation. Who would believe me if I told the truth, if I said, "It's magic."?

The best I can offer is to say that it's something like alchemy, the transformation of common metals into precious ones. That one must watch carefully, constantly, and indiscriminately and, in the watching, become a part of what is being watched. That one must see not just with sight, but taste and smell and hearing and touch. And that in the watching and becoming, words will appear and take on a life of their own.

I could offer that as an explanation, but who really believes that copper can be turned into gold?

Not long ago someone who knows me well laughed at some silliness that erupted quite unbidden from my mouth and said, "You really are still twelve years old."

Why, thank you. Thank you very much. It is, in fact, my goal in life to remain twelve (or younger) until I'm at least eighty. It would appear that I've done a pretty good job so far. And for that I credit morning moons, early tomatoes, and the good fairy.

MARCH 29, 2009

The infant spring was two days old, the back stoop was littered with the transparent pink wings of pine tree seeds, and the cars looked as though they'd been dusted with saffron. I had absolutely no business going outside and coating my lungs with what amounts to South Georgia snow, but I could stand it no longer.

Bare-legged and bare-armed I slipped out the back door and headed across the field toward the woods. Be quiet, I reminded myself, an anticipatory reprimand for the thoughts—unchangedable facts, unnecessary reminders, unimportant questions—that would, without the intervention of my mental customs agents, assail me within moments. Be quiet and listen. Listen.

Along the edge of the field road, hundreds of four-petaled white flowers hugging the ground promised blackberries in the days to come. A closer look gave me a peek at the nascent berries themselves, tight pink buds no bigger than the top of a dressmaker's pin.

Just beyond them were three dead oak trees, trunks grown together, bark fallen off in sheets, ten or twelve holes of various depths bored out by some destructive insect. How long, I wondered, did that take? And all I heard in response was that other voice reminding me to hush, to listen.

Across the pond dam I saw more blackberry blossoms, stepped over Daddy's john boat, heard birds fluttering in the underbrush like the pages of a book under a thumb. Under the arc of pine trees and scrub oaks I felt goosebumps spring up on my arms and shook my shoulders with the chill.

I'd just come down the dam and made the turn toward the low place where the creek runs along the property line when I heard a scurry that was too heavy for a bird or a field mouse. I looked off to the side and there, not more than twenty feet away, was a raccoon. He was standing up on his hind legs and holding his graceful little front paws together almost as though folded in prayer.

We exchanged a glance of intimate familiarity, like two old acquaintances, and then that voice—the one I'd done a fairly good job of silencing for the last few minutes—shrilly reminded me that if the raccoon, who shouldn't even be awake in the middle of the afternoon, had not run away immediately at the sight of me he might be rabid. So I moved on, made it in just a few more minutes to the fallen barbed wire fence I have to climb over to get into the woods proper.

I wandered around back there, crunching last winter's acorns beneath my feet and trying to keep the still-bare branches of the smaller trees from hooking themselves into my hair, for a long time. I climbed over another fence to get to a rise where I could see an adjoining piece of land planted in CRP pines and watched a loud obnoxious crow dive and loop as though believing he could convince someone he was a really a red-tailed hawk.

And I kept thinking about the raccoon. Kept seeing the eyes within the bandit's mask that reflected just enough light into their blackness for me to know he was looking at me. Kept wondering if maybe, just maybe, he had contradicted his nature and come out in the daylight because, like me, he'd been simply unable to resist the almost-gravitational pull of the change of seasons.

I walked home another way, cut through the field and came up behind the house from the other side of the pond where frogs or turtles or fish kept making shallow splashes around the submerged trunks of fallen trees. There was no need to return to the hollowed-out place in the bushes where my friend—for he was certainly by now my friend—the raccoon had taken a moment to acknowledge me. With some things, once is enough.

APRIL 12, 2009

Hallelujah! Hallelujah! Hallelujah, Hallelujah, Hallelujah!
Oh, yes, George Frideric Handel, you got it exactly right.
After days of sopping rain. After the tease of an early spring.
After the feeling that Lent would go on forever. Hallelujah!
For the azaleas that trim Savannah Avenue with a hot pink
pom-pom fringe. For the breeze that sets the branches of Mama's
Bradford pear trembling like a candle flame. For the sunrise that
reflects off the surface of the pond like a silver dollar. Hallelujah!
Sometimes one word is all it takes to express the deepest
emotion. Especially when it is a word like hallelujah, a word that
begins and ends with breath itself.

In the spring of my freshman year at Wesleyan I had Speech
with Mrs. Hatfield. It was from her clearly articulated but still
solidly Southern mouth that I learned articulatory phonetics—
bilabial, labiodental, bidental, and glottal sounds. She taught us to
say words slowly, to notice the position of tongue and teeth, to
feel the rise and fall of air with each syllable.

Mrs. Hatfield had a demonstrably proprietary interest in what
linguists call Southern American English and her own use of it
included a traditionally non-rhotic twist: The word "speaker"
came out sounding like "speakuh" and Milledgeville's most
famous literary figure was "Flannery O'Connuh." She took a very
personal offense at the impression of people in other parts of the
country that all Southerners elongated the long "I" sound and was
visibly horrified that there was someone (that would be me) in her
classroom at her fine women's college who did just that.

It was, I admit, with a great deal of pride in my South Georgia
forbears that I repeated after her, "It's a nice night out tonight."
She did not, as I recall, ask me anything about white rice.

Despite that, I was enraptured by the process of creating the
spoken word and walked around campus, intoxicated by the scent
of Japanese magnolias, saying words out loud, noticing that my

lips pressed together to say purple, that my tongue curled to the roof of my mouth to say light and lavender and love and that my upper teeth tapped my lower lip to make the "v" sound in the latter two.

It was love that I came to feel for the spoken word, as much as I had always loved its written equivalent. I learned to listen to the stories my grandfather told around the Thanksgiving table, the memories shared by the aunts shelling peas and shucking corn, the prayers my father offered in colloquial exchange with God. I heard the life force that flowed out of their mouths like a fountain. I recognized the power.

According to Genesis, God spoke the world into existence. "Let there be light," He said, curling His own tongue against the roof of His own mouth to utter four alliterative words that changed everything. The poetry of the creative proclamation echoed over the void to send water and earth and sky settling into their places. And when that single breath enlivened the human race I can't help believing that it was more than just a puff of air, that it was a word, an invitation to join the conversation.

So now, at Easter, at the end of winter and in the brightness of spring, I can very well believe that the response to that offer, the acceptance of that invitation was probably just that one word: Hallelujah!

APRIL 26, 2009

I opened my eyes to the first blush of sunrise backlighting the tippy tops of the pines on the point. The lake water, tufted like a chenille bedspread, was brown-gray, the color of the rabbit my friend's dog had chased in the woods behind Sandhill just a few days before. Outside the French doors that opened onto the lanai, Sunday morning was waking up too, stretching and sighing and blinking her eyes.

I had not been to the lake in a long time. I had never been in this house, built on the ashes and memories of the first one. Lying on my back, I stared out at the view, but saw only an endless filmstrip of images of days and nights spent in this place—a circle of chairs around a chiminea and its corkscrew curl of smoke wending into the blue night, an old woman in a hat casting her fishing line toward the water like a spider's spinneret, a boat bumping against the dock in stormy weather.

When my friends built the first house, I gave them an angel to watch over the place when they weren't there. She was about eighteen inches high and made of terra cotta. In her outstretched hands she held a book. We hung her on the second-floor screened porch and, in a little indentation on the back, my friends left the extra key.

The fire that would eventually reduce the house to ashes left nothing—no dark skeletons of appliances, no loose coins, nothing charred but still recognizable. It was as though the entire structure had simply melted down like the Wicked Witch.

When the ground was cool enough to walk on, my friend shuffled through the ashes with a stick, stirring and poking, hoping to find something that could be saved. When the stick struck something solid, she barely dared to believe.

Reaching down into the soft blackness, covering her hands in the powdery soot, she pulled out the angel. One piece of her skirt had broken off but was lying in place. "I couldn't believe it," she told me, her voice quavering, when I finally reached her on the phone. "Nothing else was saved. Nothing. She fell two stories and was lying there face up."

Life isn't always easy. It gets busy and complicated despite good intentions. It takes its toll on our bodies and our dreams. It never ever turns out the way we imagine.

Because of that, it took me a long time to get to the new house, to open myself to the idea that different walls could hold the same hospitality, to believe that something equally good—maybe even better?—could rise from the ashes.

It took a long time, but here I was watching the same sun rise in the same spot over the same trees.

Before I left to come home, there was one thing, my friend said, that had to be done. The angel, her skirt repaired with a double portion of hot-glue gun, had to be re-hung. We debated on placement, measured and drilled and gently hoisted her up onto the nail. Just right.

We backed away for a wider perspective. The book in the angel's hands looked like an offering. "Here," she seemed to be saying. "Take what I give you." And I wondered what that might be.

"She needs a new name, I think," my friend said. "Don't you agree?"

"Absolutely," I said and stared at her for a moment before turning to say, "Her new name is Phoenix."

Smile.

At the very bottom, at the edge of Phoenix's hem, there was missing a small triangular piece, so small that it had most likely been crushed by her fall. "I wish so much I'd been able to find that little piece," my friend sighed.

"I don't," I told her. "None of us goes through a fire completely unchanged. That is a reminder."

It took me a long time to get to the new house and, like Phoenix, I am not unchanged. I am, I think, better. And for that I can thank the fire.

MAY 10, 2009

It's all one big story.

Life, that is.

In rare transcendent moments of immense joy or pain, we know it. But in the ordinary moments—when the babysitter is late or the tire blows out on the interstate or the line at the grocery store is held up because the woman with three children can't find her debit card in the duffel bag she calls a purse—we tend to lose sight of that truth.

Which is why this story, the one I am about to tell you, needs telling.

In January, I drove to Savannah with Daddy to keep an appointment I'd made with the StoryCorps bus. He wasn't all that keen on the idea of sitting inside an Airstream trailer for forty-five minutes while I asked him questions about his childhood, but I reminded him that his is the last generation who grew up as the children of sharecroppers and that that way of life needed to be remembered and appreciated. It didn't hurt that I am his only daughter and, except for mouse-trap emptying, I generally don't ask for much.

So we went to Savannah and he answered my questions, told me what it was like growing up on land that did not and would not ever belong to you, raising crops that did not and would not ever belong to you. He talked about the REA and electricity and neighbors gathered around the radio. And he told the story of a black man named Del who farmed for the same man as my grandfather and who was given a nearly dead hog which he nursed back to health only to have the hog taken away by the boss man. Del's stoic response to the injustice was taught to every one of us cousins as an admonition to keep one's word: "Mr. Bowen, he make a chillun' trade."

Last Thursday both Daddy and I got calls from a nice young lady at StoryCorps in New York City. She called to tell us that a portion of the interview was going to be broadcast on NPR's Morning Edition on Friday morning. I don't know how Daddy reacted, but when I hung up the phone I went running up and down the halls of the office in my high heels screaming, "My daddy is going to be on NPR!!! Oh, my gosh, my daddy is going to be on NPR!!!"

It is unfortunate, but not necessarily germane to the story, that Georgia Public Broadcasting preempted Friday's StoryCorps segment for a fund-raising plea, a programming faux pas which meant that friends and family who had turned their dials to 91.1 FM (a station that at least some of them, prior to Friday, didn't know existed) heard only two men engaged in a slightly goofy conversation about pledges and thank-you gifts. However, those in Atlanta, South Carolina, and Maryland all heard the segment and were as delighted as I with the result. And all day on Friday I got phone calls and e-mails from people who had managed to find the web link and listen on their computers. It was a glorious day.

Five days later I got an e-mail from my high school friend Francie. We don't see each other much. Francie is a professor at a university in Virginia and her parents don't live in Statesboro anymore, so her visits here are rare. E-mail is our way of remaining a part of each other's lives.

It happened that Francie was in New York City on Friday to deliver a lecture and was staying with a friend who has a thirtieth-floor apartment overlooking the Metropolitan Opera and Lincoln Center. She wrote: "As I was blow-drying my hair the bathroom door was cracked so I could hear the radio which had NPR on, and so when I heard the strong Southern accent (which I never hear anywhere, but certainly not in New York) I, as always, tried to place from which state the speaker must be. THEN I heard the female interviewer and thought, 'That sure sounds like Kathy Bradley.' When they reintroduced the speakers at the end of the piece, I came shooting out of that bathroom screaming at the top of my lungs, 'Tony, I know those people! They're from home!'"

I cried, of course. Cried because after all this time and in such odd circumstances she recognized our voices. Cried because for Francie this will always be home and because she still understands what it means to be "from" somewhere. Cried because, as I said, it's all one story.

Once, when I was at Wesleyan, Mama and Daddy came up to hear some speaker and at the end of the program, which must not have impressed him much, Daddy said to me, "I wish somebody would give me that opportunity. If they would let me, I'd stand on the White House steps and speak to the entire nation. And I'd tell them the truth."

It wasn't the White House steps and it took about thirty years, but the entire nation did hear him. And every word of it was truth.

MAY 24, 2009

The woods that trimmed the edges of the two-lane highway were veiled in the dull light of an overcast sky. The grass and the leaves were still in the heaviness of a threatened rainstorm. Mine was the only car on the road that rolled ahead in easy waves.

While I thought about people and places far away, two squirrels came darting out of the ditch directly in front of the car. How odd, I thought in the split second it took them to cross into my lane, that two would have started across together, one leading, the other following.

The first one scurried (scurrying being the only mode of perambulation a squirrel has in his repertoire) straight across the road and disappeared into the high grass on the other side. The second squirrel, the follower, got almost all the way across, stopped, stood up on his back legs and unexplainably, yet not surprisingly, turned to go back the other way.

I couldn't stop. Had not enough time to slow down or even swerve to miss him. It took less than three seconds. I looked in my rearview mirror and saw only a small dark spot near the white center-line.

Then I heard myself talking to the squirrel. "Why did you do that? Why didn't you just keep going? You started across; you would have made it! Crazy squirrel!"

And another voice, my same voice, but the one that knows things, said, "It's all about risk."

The stack of board games in our house growing up included Monopoly and Clue and Scrabble. We had a Parchesi at one point and checkers, both regular and Chinese. And after three Christmases of asking, I finally got a Barbie - Queen of the Prom game. What we didn't have, never had, was Risk.

In its red box on the shelf at McConnell's Dime Store, it never became the object of my interest or desire. Even then, at eight and ten and twelve, I wanted a sure thing. I wanted guarantees, promises, absolute assurances.

For a long time it worked. I played only those games I knew I could win, spent my time on things I knew I could do well, set my sights on goals that were easily within my grasp. But somewhere along the way I realized that something was missing. I realized that I wasn't growing and I wasn't having any fun.

What I also realized was that the only way to do either of those things was to stop hoarding my Monopoly money, stop solving make-believe murders, and stop dressing for a pretend prom. It was time to take a few chances.

Since then I've been each of the squirrels at various times. I've been the first squirrel and made it across the highway, heart racing, limbs trembling, and grinning from ear to ear. And I've been the second squirrel, the one who froze in fear and tried to return to the old place, only to be crushed by something big and loud.

I have been exhilarated and deliriously happy. I have been despondent and desperately disappointed. I have been warmly content and I have been coldly morose. And every moment of every emotion has been infinitely better than the lethargy of being a little metal thimble making its way around a cardboard square over and over and over again.

Each morning we wake up on one side of the highway. Some days it's good to just roll over and stare up at the flotilla of gauzy white clouds. On other days, though, the breeze and the sunlight and the smell of something pleasant that we can't quite identify lure us to the edge of the asphalt. And on those days, there is simply nothing left to do except run headlong into the open.

JUNE 7, 2009

The dressing rooms on the second floor of Minkovitz Department Store were poorly lit and small, just big enough for a narrow stool and the floor space for one person to dress and undress. To get a full view of whatever it was that one was trying on, one had to leave the dressing room and walk out onto the sales floor where God and the sales ladies and, worst of all, possibly somebody popular who was also shopping could see how tight the skirt was through the hips or how inadequately the bodice was filled.

I was subjected to this torture only a few times as, for all the hours I spent in a Minkovitz dressing room, we—Mama and I— never had any serious intention of actually buying anything.

I take that back: Mama never had any intention; I was always hopeful.

From the day Mama and Daddy brought me home from the old red brick hospital on Grady Street, whatever I wore was homemade, floating forth from under the presser foot of Mama's Singer sewing machine in a froth of soft cotton batiste, crisp gingham, and velvety corduroy. The Peter Pan collars on my church dresses were finished in double-stitched scallops and the tiniest of pin tucks framed rows of shiny pearl buttons down the fronts.

Somewhere around second grade I figured out that not everyone dressed the way that I did. Some of them had skirts that looked exactly alike. They had small satin tags sewn into their necklines and, occasionally, some writing or an animal on the outside. And, because the need to be "like" and "liked" arises early in girls, it was somewhere around second grade that I began to resent the fact that none of my clothes came from Minkovitz or Belk or—Be still, my heart.—The Children's Shop.

By the time I got to junior high, Mama, who just couldn't justify spending money on clothes that were not as well-made as the ones she sewed, and I had reached a compromise: We went shopping, just like all my friends, dragging an armload of skirts and blouses and dresses into the dressing room, plastic hangers clicking and getting tangled together. I tried each outfit on and stood very still while Mama, pulling out her little Blue Horse top-bound spiral notebook, drew detailed pictures of what I was wearing.

She made notes like "grosgrain ribbon trim" and drew arrows to the place on the dress where said trim would be placed. She rubbed the fabric between her knowledgeable hands and then wrote "polyester and cotton" or "100% wool." She drew every detail—square pockets and notched collars and two-inch cuffs.

After closing the notebook, dropping it back down into her patent leather purse that closed with a loud click, and gathering up all the clearly not-up-to-snuff garments, Mama would walk out to meet the sales ladies while I dressed. Through the heavy fabric curtain at the dressing room door I could hear her say, "No, we didn't find anything today."

An hour later we would be leaving the fabric store weighted down with a Simplicity or Butterick pattern, a couple of yards of fabric folded into a nice square with a paper tag pinned to the top, thread, zipper, buttons, and sometimes elastic, all of which would go into the magician's hat that was Mama's creativity and be transformed into an infinitely better version of what I had been craving since the moment I saw it on the rack at the department store.

I was not so wise at thirteen to recognize the gift of a mother who could work this magic. I did not always have the most pleasant attitude as I sat on the stool at the counter flipping through the pages of the pattern books to find the one that most closely resembled what I'd just tried on. I did not, as I recall, one single time ever tell Mama that I appreciated what she did.

I didn't because I didn't. I didn't tell her because I didn't appreciate it. I had not the capacity yet to understand that love comes in a profusion of forms, in astonishingly different ways, and through surprisingly odd vehicles. I had not the experience yet to know that love is not simply affection, devotion or desire, but the choice to be moved into action by it.

I didn't then. I do now.

JUNE 21, 2009

I opened the car door and turned to get out. My breath hit the still, hot air like an egg hits simmering water and hovered there— poached oxygen. My arms were instantly damp and sticky and my clothes, light and comfortable that morning when I put them on, suddenly collapsed onto my skin like Saran Wrap. I forced my bare feet onto the concrete of the carport and felt a brief moment of relief.

June in South Georgia. Ah, yes.

I gathered up the mail and my briefcase and my gym bag and the shoes I'd kicked off the moment I'd left the office. Arms full, brain distracted, I started toward the back steps.

Something moved. Just a little something, but enough. I stopped. Squinted my eyes. A snake. Stretched out his full length along one of the steps, his pointy little head raised up toward the clapboards, reconnoitering a possible breach whereby he might invade my sanctuary.

My heart clutched just a second. I quietly set down my burdens, forgetting for a moment that the audacious reptile couldn't hear, and backed away toward the only weapon anywhere close.

I pulled the hosepipe from its wheel, turned on the faucet, and began an aqueous assault that would have made any seaman proud. Water firing toward his head in a violent stream, the snake turned slowly away from the wall and inched bit by bit down the steps. It took at least five minutes to herd him off the carport, through the hostas and under the deck.

Only then, less than three feet from the deck, did I see the two additional snakes, twined together around the deck post just outside the bedroom door, a live caduceus. I turned the spray toward them. This time it took longer.

When the immediate crisis was past and they were dangling from the other side of the deck, twisting and turning like exotic dancers, I did what I always do: I went for Daddy.

Within ten minutes, the two deck snakes had been sent to their reward by deadly-accurate shotgun blasts. (The first, I truly believe, was prayed away by my friend Mandy who had called in the midst of the initial assault.) The friend I call Mr. Green Jeans has reprimanded me for my malevolent reaction, reminded me that those snakes feed on the mice that I hate even more, and accused me of disturbing the delicate ecosystem around Sandhill.

Sorry. It's just that, well, I don't like interlopers. I don't like my security being breached. I don't like being reminded of my vulnerability.

None of us do. We pretend to embrace our humanness with its inherent fragility. We pose as sensitive creatures who are moved to tears by sunsets and big-eyed puppies and giggling toddlers, but it's all a sham. And it lasts only until the snake crawls out of the branch and stretches out across the path blocking the way. At that moment, whether the snake is a reptile or another human being posing as one, what every one of us wants to be is bullet-proof and Teflon-coated, an unshakeable monolith inspiring the awe and respect of weaker souls.

Good luck.

Because what we all have to ultimately admit is that there are no bullet-proof, Teflon-coated people. And there are no impenetrable walls. The best for which any of us can hope is to have within reaching distance another soul with a shotgun or, better yet, an available pray-er.

JULY 5, 2009

In June even the lowest tide is still high, making the beach a narrow ribbon of eggshell-colored sand. And so it was that there was just enough room, on this dazzlingly brilliant Saturday afternoon, for a few rows of white folding chairs, a line of serious men in black tuxedos, a loop of pretty girls in diaphanous pink dresses, and, of course, the bride.

The walk down to the beach from the hotel, in high-heeled mules that click-clacked on the asphalt like miniature jack-hammers, had not taken long. There had been no breeze on the street and moving through the two o'clock, 105-degree heat had been like pushing through an endless succession of heavy curtains.

But here at the edge of the water, where the waves spread out in thin pancakes and the rocks over to the side caught the sound of rushing water and rolled it back out in a sustained whisper, it was almost possible—almost—to forget the trickle of sweat that rolled down my sternum.

I waited, there on the second row with the grandmother, for the guitar music to start and for people I love so much it makes me ache to walk down the narrow aisle of sand. I tried to concentrate on the present moment, not the nearly twenty-seven years of moments that had brought my Adam to his wedding day.

The old, old ritual moved through its steps. The words were repeated. The hands were joined. The flower girls dropped petals from their chubby hands and watched the sea breeze waft them away. At one point the minister stepped forward as the ocean slid under his shoes and, following his lead, the black tuxedos and pink dresses did the same.

And then it was over. Jenn and Adam, sporting new jewelry and smiles that came from somewhere deep inside, walked out together, hand in hand.

What followed—the posing for photographs, the hugging of the same people over and over again, the repetitive but completely sincere declarations of how beautiful the bride, how handsome the groom, how hot the weather—left us tired and sated with happiness.

A week later, the photographer (a good friend of mine) sent me a few sneak peeks of the photos while the newlyweds were still in the Bahamas. I teared up over the one of Daddy helping Adam with his cuff links. I lost my breath over the one of me and beautiful, grown-up Kate. I giggled at the one of Adam skipping down the street, dragging Jenn along, bubbles floating in the air around them.

But there was one—a black and white—that told the story, that preached the sermon, that spoke all the unspeakable words. Adam and Jenn, hands clasped, are looking not at each other but over the shoulder of the minister at the advancing tide. Their faces show no worry, no discomfort, no concern that the rented tux or the ethereal white dress might get stained or damaged. There is no question about whether they should move to avoid the watery licks at their feet. There is no panic, just interest.

Anyone who has ever watched a beloved child grow up and choose a partner has done it with a catch in the throat, a breath held just slightly, wondering if what that child has learned about life and love and commitment will be enough to carry him or her through the days to come. Anyone who has ever made the promises knows how hard they are to keep. Anyone who has ever prayed prays on that day that the inevitable difficulties will be just hard enough to build strength, not so hard as to scar.

This is what I am thinking as I stare at the photograph—the one of my Adam and, now, my Jenn—over and over again. And in the staring I see them not just standing on the beach, but standing on the threshold of their life together—without fear, holding on to each other and looking in the same direction. It is, I think, a very good way to start.

JULY 19, 2009

The early evening breeze, making its way through the cornfield whose stalks are now fading from bright green to dull gold, sounds like an advancing rain shower and I have to look up from my book to figure out which it is. No water, just wind. Soft and easy it comes across the yard, so gently that the wind chimes hanging from the eaves over my head do not move, so gently that the thin leaves on the chinaberry tree vibrate no more than a blinking eyelash; so gently that the single hummingbird can float before the feeder, hesitate a moment as though she's never seen such a thing before, and then tilt her head slightly to plunge her beak into the fake flower like a needle into silk.

It has been a busy summer. A summer of weddings and parties and warm times with people I love. All good things. But there have been few moments of inactivity, few moments to sit on the deck and watch the hummingbirds. The feeders emptied last week without my noticing and I refilled them this morning with more than a dash of guilt and a whispered prayer for absolution. The birds, at least this one, seem to have forgiven me.

The larger question is whether I've forgiven myself.

Nothing has been neglected really. Nothing except the hummingbirds and the hanging baskets of petunias that, let's face it, never really stood a chance in the constant heat. I've managed to make the telephone calls to keep the grass cut. I've sent all the birthday and anniversary cards for June and July. I picked enough blackberries to make a few pints of jam.

And yet in this moment, with my legs stretched out on the lawn chair, my hand curved around a glass of tea, and my breath easier than it's been in weeks, I understand that what I've snubbed with my busyness, what I've slighted in my constant movement, what I've disregarded in my attention to the details of my to-do lists, is myself.

A couple of weeks ago I was having a conversation with someone who knows me well. We were speaking of esoteric things, peculiar ideas and polarizing opinions, unanswerable questions and undoubtable truths. I think—no, I'm sure—I was being deliberately obtuse. I wanted to talk, but my brain was too tired. I wanted to engage, but I was physically and mentally incapable of doing so. At some point, frustrated like an infant needing a nap, I replied to a particular question with a harsh, "I don't know!"

I expected a reprimand. Or something along the lines of, "Sure you do." Or something that would allow me to rev up the tension, complain about the busyness of my life and elicit some sympathy.

What I got instead was, "Be still and know. You have to be still to know."

Ouch.

So now it's Saturday. The perennials I spent the morning planting smile at me from the flower bed at the bottom of the deck steps. The sycamore tree whose bottom limbs, puddling on the grass, I'd trimmed away with Mama's hacksaw sighs deeply with the extra breathing room. The hummingbird hums, sucking at the Kool-Aid in the hourglass-shaped feeder.

And I am being still.

Still and noticing that the sun is setting in a slightly different place than the last time I watched. Noticing that the kudzu on the trees in the branch between the house and the pond has completely obscured the view of the water. Noticing that my skin is browner, that there are no mosquitoes, that the humidity isn't so bad.

I am being still and I can feel myself contracting and expanding: contracting to expel the waste of used-up energy, expanding to take in the pulse-beat of everything around me. Breathing out the hurry, breathing in the calm.

I am being still and, in the stillness, I know everything I need to know.

AUGUST 2, 2009

Late afternoon. Sun low in the sky, kissing the tops of buildings in the distance. Tide going out in choppy waves.

Daphne and I are sitting on the beach, arms and shoulders and legs exposed to the still-warm air, eyes shielded by dark glasses. We have been inside all day listening to serious and dedicated people talk about the hard things our job forces us to see and hear and try to understand. We have been inundated with images of pain and evil. We have been reminded of the existence of worlds we will never know.

But now, outside absorbing the sunlight, we are simply admiring each other's swimsuits, making plans for dinner, and talking about life. Talking about it as though we can actually make sense of it, as though we can actually anticipate the future with enough accuracy to be prepared for it, as though we can actually shield ourselves from the possibilities of pain and evil.

To one side of us is a young couple taking down a beach tent, obviously well-practiced as they position themselves at opposite corners and release the latches in unison. On the hard-packed sand near the edge of the water are a handful of young boys, long-legged and skinny, trying to tame the wind and fly kites. Behind us is an elaborate sand castle, molded not by small hands but by turret-shaped plastic buckets.

I absorb it all without being distracted from the conversation, keep my attention on the story Daphne is telling me, offer sensitive and cogent interjections at just the right moments. And then I realize that I have turned my head toward the water, that I am watching something other than my friend's expressive face.

Just off the beach is a windsurfer struggling with his sail. A little farther downwind is another having no better luck. Neither one is particularly skilled. Both are managing to remain upright, but there is no fluidity in their movements, no grace in their maneuvers. They are so close to the shore than I cannot imagine that they are experiencing much in the way of transcendence. I feel sorry for them.

I don't windsurf. But I have spent hours watching it. I can recognize the pure pleasure that comes from skimming the waves, leaning into the wind and letting it carry board and body and sail through air that smells of sun and salt. These two, the strugglers, are not experiencing that pleasure.

The next night I am talking to my friend the windsurfer, the one from whom I learned what I know, and I tell him about it. "Why," I ask him, "would they be staying so close to shore? That can't be much fun."

"What was the direction of the wind?" he asks.

I try to remember, tell him where I'd been sitting, figure out that the wind was blowing in.

"That's it," he says. "To get farther out they would have had to fight the wind. Not everyone wants to work that hard."

Instant gratification. Quick fix. It is what, unfortunately, most of us prefer.

"You put in the effort first," he goes on. "Tack, then sail."

Of course. That is the secret. Put all your energy—ALL your energy—into the climb, then trust gravity to bring you safely down. Put all your effort into the living, then trust life to bring you what you want. Tack, then sail.

The late summer light fades while we talk and I sit in near-darkness. I can close my eyes and I still see the two figures, tense and stiff, knees and elbows locked. I can almost hear the release of tightly-held breaths as their boards strike sand.

And I think about sitting on the beach with Daphne, working on our tans and our lives. I know what I will tell her when I see her again, the next time we find ourselves asking questions and wondering what is ahead.

"It's all pretty simple," I will say. "Tack, then sail."

AUGUST 16, 2009

Lily is a good dog. She loves to go with me when I walk or run down the long dusty roads at Sandhill. She growls alertly at anything or anyone she deems suspicious and she generally comes when she is called.

She lets you know that she wants to be petted by lifting her left front paw and patting whatever part of your body is within reach. She likes to have her belly scratched, but is willing to settle for a quick pass with the bottom of my shoe. She has the square jaw of at least one boxer relative somewhere in her genetic past and when she smiles the lower cuspid on one side of her mouth sticks out over her upper lip, making her looking a little like Popeye.

Lily is a good dog. And I love her.

But I have not forgotten Ginny.

And sometimes, when I see the long face and sunshine-colored hair of someone else's golden retriever, my heart clutches just slightly and for a moment I am sitting on the laundry room floor, holding Ginny in my lap, crying over some heartbreak and wiping my eyes with her silky ears.

You never get over your first dog.

Which is why, this morning, already running a little bit late, I had no choice but to pick him up.

I'd come to the stop sign at Highway 301 and, looking to the left for oncoming traffic, saw this glorious golden retriever loping along the side of the too-busy highway. He walked straight up to the car (Goldens are like that: they trust everyone and believe with all their hearts that everyone loves them.) as though he'd been expecting me.

I got out and reached for his collar, one of those flourescent orange ones with the brass nameplates, the kind that hunters use. This was seen as an invitation to frolic and he began licking my hands and dancing around my legs, wiping me with the dirt and dew that his fur had collected in his wanderings.

Realizing that I'd never be able to read a name or telephone number off his collar unless he was confined, I opened the back door of the car and he jumped right in. I called the number, left a message, and turned around to take him back to our farm where he could safely await his master.

It took less than ten minutes and, while I drove, I thought about Ginny. This dog was lighter in color, bigger in size, a male. Not really much in common with Ginny, except the breed. And that was enough. Enough to let me know that I didn't need to be afraid of him and that he would gladly accept my kindness.

It occurs to me people are like dogs in that way: We each have our breed. Some of us are chihuahuas, in constant motion, nipping at the heels of anything that moves, yapping constantly. Some of us are poodles, delicate and high-strung. Some of us are boxers with imposing physical presences and Forrest Gump personalities. And, just like dogs, while we'll travel in a pack of pretty much any combination, we'd really rather be with some of our own.

Just as I was getting my new friend into the dog pen his master returned my call, got directions, and started our way. I backed the car up and started for the office for the second time this morning.

I didn't realize until later that I'd not noticed his name. It was on the collar, along with his master's name and telephone number, but I hadn't noticed it. It didn't matter. I knew his breed and that was enough.

AUGUST 30, 2009

I was standing in chest-high water, the waves slapping at my back like love licks. Behind me was the wide wide ocean; in front of me was a watercolored beach—white sand, red lifeguard chair, scattered people in various shades of pink and brown stretched out under the sun that came down in wavy yellow beams. My friend had left me to become one of those toasting people and so I was alone at the moment, a tiny island just offshore.

It had been a busy weekend—another wedding!—and I was hungry for space. The sand slid and shifted under my toes, which I had curled tightly in an effort to keep my balance. Hands on my hips, chin tilted toward the sky, I took a deep breath.

At just that moment, a pair of pelicans entered the frame of my vision, flying so low I could make out the line where their dark cartilaginous beaks meshed with their jiggly white pouches. I had never been that close to pelicans, never seen them flying so near people. I was startled, but not frightened. They appeared to be neither. And with a couple of flaps of long brown wings they were gone, the encounter over, the moment past.

There are some things that evoke praise, some things that draw forth an eruption of amazement, some things that—rather than take your breath—give you an explosion of breath that pours out in a rolling swell of words. There are some moments when silence is blasphemy.

This was one of those moments. And so it was that I stood there in the shallows of the endless sea and heard a voice that was clearly mine making exclamations of how very glad I was to be alive, how very grateful I was for the serendipity of pelicans flying low, how very much I wanted to make sure that I squeezed out of that day and every day all that was meant to be mine.

It is, I think, pretty much irrelevant to whom I was speaking—to myself or to the pelicans or to God. What matters is that the words came of their own accord, without hesitation and without editing. What matters is that those small puffs of wind were expelled into and absorbed by the larger wind that makes the waves that make the tides that make the sand into which my toes kept uselessly digging.

I opened my eyes, which I had closed momentarily, to see a boy, eleven or twelve years old, standing about twenty-five feet away between me and the beach. He was looking at me. He was looking at me quizzically. He was looking at me as though he wasn't sure whether to pretend he didn't see me or to turn and run as fast as he could.

I realized, too late, of course, that the wind—the one that makes the waves and tides—was blowing in. In toward the beach. In toward where he was standing. And, yes, the poor child had heard my spontaneous invocation. I can only imagine what he was thinking.

I gave up the bad habit of allowing myself to be embarrassed a long time ago. There is absolutely no value to it and it takes far too much time and energy. I didn't, then, feel my face turn red nor did I have an urge to look around as though I, too, had heard something strange and did not know from whence it came. I just looked at him, made as much eye contact as one can from that distance, and watched him, in his pre-adolescent suspicion, scope out his mother a little farther down the beach and begin moving in her direction.

It was funny. Really. I am laughing still. Laughing at how silly I must have looked (I think I probably raised my hands at some point) and sounded. Laughing at how astonished the boy was, his eyes and mouth frozen into three big circles. Laughing at how foolish we are to think that we odd creatures are ever anything but funny.

I waited a few minutes and then slogged my way through the water up onto the beach where I shook out a towel, stretched out, and joined the rest of the pink and brown people—all of us different, all of us funny, all of us laughing in short sweet breaths of wind.

SEPTEMBER 13, 2009

It still surprises me that people who have known me for, let's say, less than thirty years, all seem to assume that I grew up on the farm, that my ability to identify coffee weed appeared along with my baby teeth, that the first motorized vehicle I drove was a tractor, and that I know how to birth baby pigs. The truth is that I was a reluctant transplant to Adabelle, seventeen years old and counting down the days before I left for college.

In those eight months and in the holidays over the next seven years, however, I managed to obtain an accelerated education. I learned to chase runaway cows and move pigs from one pen to another. I learned what a soybean was and made a reasonable effort to understand something called soybean futures. I climbed grain bins, rode tractors, experienced something akin to quicksand by playing in a trailer of just-combined corn. I watched the skies and prayed for rain.

None of those things are remarkable anymore. They are a part of the rhythm of my days.

The other day I was in the backyard making a new flower bed, pulling out long white fingers of grass roots from the dry gray dirt, and looked up toward the road at an unusually loud truck rattle. Daddy was pulling the corn auger from the shed up to the grain bin.

The auger is tall and skinny and looks like a praying mantis made of sheet metal. One end goes into the grain bin and another into the truck holding shelled corn. In one of those amazing feats of mechanical engineering that I don't understand, the auger twirls 'round and 'round and draws the corn up its narrow neck and into the bin. Sure beats shoveling.

I stopped my digging long enough to watch the slow procession—Daddy with his elbow hanging out the open truck window, getting him closer to the rearview mirror to make sure that the auger did not veer off into the adjacent fields—and remembered hearing for the first time, during that first overwhelming summer, somebody mention an auger.

My thoughts—the thoughts of the bookish literary-minded girl I was—had gone immediately to *Julius Caesar* and the warning of the priests whose auguring ("Plucking the entrails of an offering forth/They could not find a heart within the beast.") convinced them that Caesar should avoid the Senate on that day. Different word, different spelling, but my only frame of reference.

Thirty-five years later, my own hands plunged deep into dirt, not animal entrails, I found myself laughing at possible confusion between the two words, the idea that an auger could foretell the future, that the waterfall of bright gold kernels splashing into a grain bin could divine tomorrow, that the cloud of corn pollen that rises and falls in a fine layer on grass and sleeves and eyelashes is some sort of pixie dust.

But, of course, it can. Of course, it is. Just as an auger curls its way up into the sky, so Daddy's choice to bring us all here, to the dirt road and the scrub oaks and the wide open sky, curled its way into our thinking, bore into our definition of what is good and right, twirled itself so tightly into our vision of how things should be that it—after a while—seemed no longer a choice, but destiny.

We like choice. We like to think that we have control. We like moving down the line at the sandwich shop and telling the disinterested young man in the corporate-logo'ed shirt that we'd like lettuce, tomato, no onions, just a few cucumbers, and light mayo on one of fifty-something possible combinations of meat and bread.

And that is a comfort. But it is also a comfort to sit in the sun on a clear September day and hear the wind chimes sing in the breeze through the chinaberry tree and be glad, be oh so very glad, that some things are just meant to be.

SEPTEMBER 27, 2009

It is hard not to think of it as my road or, at the very least, our road, my and my family's road. No one else was living on this five-mile stretch of sticky clay and powdery dirt when we took up residence here and, to this day, long after other residents have acquired an address on the road Daddy named, I still look up at the sound of a passing vehicle assuming that it is somehow connected to us.

I have walked hundreds of miles between the ditches that the county drags sometimes, crossing tracks made by deer and turtles and snakes and birds of Lord-knows-how-many species. I have pulled a young Adam and even younger Kate in a little red wagon over the undulating bumps created by farm machinery. I have foolishly punished myself by riding a bicycle through sand that provided no traction.

Sandhill sits about halfway between the two paved roads that are the bookends for our dirt one. When I get into the car and head out I don't have to pay a whole lot of attention. I've driven that two-mile stretch in every kind of weather and I know exactly when to slow down, speed up, move over. My hands and feet respond to memory without any specific direction from my brain, which is then free to wander. I can go through the day's to-do list or lose myself in an NPR piece. I can notice the morning sunlight coming through the pine trees like a laser and smile at my good fortune.

And in about four minutes I can find myself at the stop sign, scanning the county road for pickup trucks going the back way to the poultry plant, before pulling out onto the hardtop. Except that several times lately I've been jerked from my reverie by something totally unexpected.

Our neighbors up on the highway farm a couple of the fields on either side of our dirt road. And they irrigate those fields regularly. At least five or six times this summer I have come smoothly around the bad curve on dry and dusty road only to find my tires suddenly slipping and sliding into muddy clay. I've not ended up in a ditch yet, but it's been close a time or two and less than charitable words have slipped out of my mouth as I've maneuvered the car away from a vertical drop of three feet or more.

The last time it happened I felt the tightening of my muscles and the flood of adrenaline and, then, equally as unexpected as the slipping and sliding, came the flash of insight. It is, as I thought, my road. But it is subject to the conditions all around it. And those conditions aren't always created by rain or wind or other acts of God. Sometimes they are created by other people.

It is a metaphor so often used as to become predictable and trite, but it is used so often because it so applicable: Life is a road. We can plan the trip, unfold the old gas station map, or print out something from Google to plot the course. We can fill the tank, check the oil and the tire pressure, clean the windshield of squashed bugs. We can get a good night's rest and pack some snacks. With the help of the Weather Channel, we can even accelerate or postpone the journey to take advantage of optimum atmospheric conditions.

What we cannot do is predict the behavior of other people. Drivers, passengers, pedestrians. DOT engineers waving flags, farmers irrigating fields. The homeless woman pushing the grocery cart, the biker in the funny-looking helmet and Spandex shorts. They slow us down, create road hazards, force us onto detours, and—let's face it—very seldom know or care that their actions affect our journeys.

So it's up to me and me alone to make sure I don't go crashing through a barricade or running over a two-by-four. It's up to me to pay close enough attention to the changes around me that I don't end up in the ditch. It's my road, but there are other people on it. And, if I want to get home, I have to share.

OCTOBER 11, 2009

I saw autumn once. Real autumn. Cloudless sky the color of delphiniums. Trees that moved in the breeze like flamenco dancers, skirts flounced in leaves the red of the ripest plums, the gold of a long-worn wedding band, the orange of new rust. Creek water already so cold it raised the hair on my arms as I dragged my fingers through its ripples.

It was in New England, the first week in October, and I wore turtlenecks and a jacket that was supposed to look like an old Indian blanket. I picked up leaves and pressed them between the pages of the notebook I carried.

I found myself thinking in cliches—describing the air as "brisk," as though it had legs and could move them quickly—and taking far too many photographs of the same colorful trees over and over. I decided I liked apple cider.

And when I got home, walked off the plane taking off my jacket so I could breathe, I was feeling a little—yes, I admit it—a little ashamed of this place where most of the trees stay green and nobody taps maple trees for sugar and my turtlenecks wouldn't be needed for at least another couple of months.

Pure silliness.

Autumn, of course, comes to South Georgia as surely as it comes to New England; it just looks different. Instead of flushing the landscape with the entire spectrum, it carries a single paintbrush laden with one color, the bright yellow of French's mustard—goldenrod at every crossroad, at the base of every light pole, on the line of every fence row. Happy-faced asters and soft-edge primroses, foxglove and buttercups. They do not dance; they just sway to the music of the still-warm breeze through the pine trees like the homely girl in the corner at the homecoming dance.

And it doesn't make a whole lot of fuss either. It casually saunters in while everybody's attention is on getting the corn out of the fields and planning for the first tailgate. One morning you walk outside, feel a little shiver in your shoulders, and suddenly have a craving for turnips.

Then it's time for the fair and cane syrup and while you're there somebody invites you to a peanut boiling and, before you know it, the newspaper is running that unscramble-the-names-and-win-a-turkey promotion and it's Thanksgiving.

No, it's not the autumn of elementary school bulletin boards or Charles Kuralt's video essays, but it is autumn nonetheless. Our autumn.

Last week, when the moon was nearly full, I lit some citronella candles out on the deck (something no New Englander would ever have to do in October) and stood in the dark staring up at the big white circle. The fields on either side of Sandhill had given up their corn and the empty stalks had been felled by a rotary cutter in preparation for dove season. The frog chorus that had been a loud accompaniment to any kind of outdoor activity all summer was faint and arrhythmic. I realized it had been several days since I'd filled the hummingbird feeders.

The season had, once again without fanfare, stolen in and settled herself.

There is a lot to be said for the absence of fanfare, for subtlety and grace, for one true color liberally applied.

OCTOBER 25, 2009

After two days of cold—days that belonged in some other month, some other state—October came home and teased me outside with the still crispness that doesn't require a jacket but makes you want to wear one anyway.

There was no wind to carry my scent or the sound of my feet shuffling in the sand, so the dogs didn't come running from the backyard where they were overseeing Mama picking up pecans until they saw me, just past the mailbox and walking away from the sunset. Lily simply fell in beside me; Tamar had to lick my hand before trotting ahead. They, like all of us, are creatures of habit.

We didn't walk very far. The dogs demanded no explanation. They simply turned when I turned.

The sun was still over the treetops but low enough to make me squint. I looked down at the sudden glint of metal in the middle of the road. Bending over to pick it up, I expected to find only one of those aluminum disks that contractors put under nail heads. It was, however, a quarter. Heads up. George Washington's profile with the straight nose and wig flipped up on the ends like a 1960s cover girl.

There are two schools of thought about found coins. One is a poem that Katherine taught me at Wesleyan: "Find a penny, pick it up, all the day you'll have good luck. Find a penny, let it lie, before the day you'll surely die." The other is less lyrical and less morbid: Picking up a penny that is lying heads up brings good luck; picking up a penny that is lying heads down brings bad luck.

The contradiction between these two points of common wisdom is intriguing. According to the first, picking up a penny that you finding lying heads down will result in good fortune for a day. According to the second, picking up that same penny will kill you.

How can both be true? They can't. Unless the finder is one who is eager to throw off the garment of flesh and exchange it for whatever form awaits in the next life.

Which points out the problem with common wisdom: that, while it may very well be common in a "generally known" sense, it is rarely common in a "shared by all" sense. And, of course, superstition isn't wisdom at all. Or is it?

I slowed my pace and rubbed the quarter with my thumb, ran it through my fingers like a magician, thought about flipping into the nearly-dusk sky and changed my mind immediately at the panic of trying to find it again if I dropped it. Without a pocket, I had to close my fingers around it if I wanted to keep it.

And I did want to keep it, didn't I? I'd found it. It was mine now, wasn't it? I could drop it in the milk bottle where I put all my quarters. And when I had 560 I could buy that turntable at Best Buy. And then I could start over again and when I got 720 more I could buy the new tuner that matched.

Back at the house, I dropped the quarter on the kitchen counter and started supper.

Now it's on my desk and in the lamplight I can see it better. I can see the ribbon at the end of George's ponytail and I can read "liberty" in all capital letters in the rainbow curve over his head.

Suddenly, I have an idea. Excuse me for a minute.

...

Okay. I'm back.

This is what I did: I walked outside and tramped out into the edge of the branch as far as I dared go in the dark and I threw the quarter into that dark. I heard it fall, hit leaves that had themselves fallen.

Common wisdom says that a penny or, in this case, a quarter saved is a quarter earned.

Sometimes. But not tonight.

NOVEMBER 8, 2009

There is a finite number of full moons in a person's life. Fairly obvious and at the same time startling, the thought came to me Monday night as the light from the cream-colored poker chip in the sky spilled over my shoulder and into my lap and the miles between me and Sandhill grew fewer.

I caught my breath. Held it for a moment high in my chest. Felt my hands loosen their grip on the steering wheel just slightly as I heard the night whisper, "Pay attention."

So I did.

What I noticed first was the color of the light itself. Not white or yellow like the beam of a lightbulb, but luminous blue-green, like pool water at night. And not clear and piercing, but diffused as though coming through a scrim. There were no edges to the light, no defined stream; the entire landscape was covered and seemed to shiver under its immeasurable weight.

It was dark—the sun had been down for an hour at least—but the outlines of the houses, the barns, the fences, the billboards were all still clean and straight, like portraiture silhouettes.

Turning onto the dirt road, the angle of the light shifted and now came through the back windshield making me feel, more than ever, as though I was being stalked. Erratic breaks in the tree canopy turned the moonlight into a strobe, flashing up and down, side to side, the color now reminding me of the blacklight posters Keith used to have on his bedroom walls.

As I pulled into the carport, the moon was straight ahead, no longer stalking but beckoning. Its light had turned the deck into a castle keep, the stark white deck posts into silver ramparts, the pots of rosemary into miniature turrets.

There were none of the usual nighttime sounds coming from the branch. The chill in the air had silenced the crickets, the frogs, the birds. The light had stilled the deer who would wait until later to forage the now-empty fields for some last vestige of corn hidden in the trampled-over rows. I was as alone as one ever is.

I like to think that I always pay attention. I like to think that my eyes and my mind are always open. I like to think that I always notice things of beauty and matters of import. But none of those things are always true. Sometimes I'm just plain lazy.

Not lazy in the sense of neglecting work or responsibility, but lazy in letting work and responsibility overwhelm the reality that nobody lives forever, beauty is fleeting, relationships need tending.

Sometimes I read three pages of a book and realize I don't know what I've read or catch myself singing along with something on the radio and realize I've just said/sung something I don't believe to be true. Sometimes I put a stamp on a birthday card without remembering the face of the person to whom it is being sent and breathing a prayer of gratitude for that life. Sometimes I look out the window and realize that the season has changed and I didn't notice.

That is no way to live.

There is a finite number of full moons in a person's life. A finite number of sunsets, of low tides, of tomato sandwiches, of chances to love without condition. I don't want to miss a single one.

NOVEMBER 22, 2009

I pushed back the covers and put my bare feet on the floor. I pushed my bare arms through the loose sleeves of the bathrobe and, in the familiar darkness of my own house, headed toward the front door. I walked out onto the porch and then onto the brick steps whose coolness pricked the bottoms of my feet.

It was four o'clock in the morning. I had awakened without an alarm, something about the excitement notifying my sleeping brain that it was time.

Time for the Leonids meteor shower. Time to watch the light of millions of particles flying off the tail of Comet 55 spray across the sky like paint out of an aerosol can.

I'd gone out earlier to get my bearings according to the sky-map I'd printed out from the BBC webpage. Look east; locate the Big Dipper; look to the right and there in the center of the constellation Leo I would see the celestial fireworks.

Except that I didn't.

I didn't because a froth of fog covered the entire span of sky.

I stood there for a moment while it sunk in. It had been eleven years since the comet had been this close to Earth and my chance to bend my neck into an unnatural configuration and be little-kid-amazed was lost.

Sigh. Somewhere people were gasping in wonder and smiling involuntarily at the spectacle. Somewhere people were pointing and grabbing elbows. Somewhere people were watching the night explode. But not here.

The air's cool dampness wrapped around me like the strips of an old sheet we might have used to turn ourselves into mummies on Halloween. I was paralyzed with the frustration of not getting what I wanted. I felt the dew wetting my feet, but I couldn't move.

I was the petulant child who crosses her arms and stomps her feet and sticks out her lip in the distorted belief that what she wants actually matters.

But no amount of stomping or pouting was going to move the fog and, eventually, I turned around and went back inside.

Disappointment. It is such a palpable emotion.

Near the beginning of the movie *The Big Chill*, a group of college friends gathers for the funeral of one of their circle. They walk into the church together while one of them goes to the organ to play. She spreads her fingers to reach the notes of the beginning chords and, while the congregation and the audience anticipates which of the standard funeral hymns she will offer, they hear instead the opening measures of The Rolling Stones's "You Can't Always Get What You Want."

It is an unexpected moment of comic relief and, simultaneously, a heartbreaking declaration of truth.

We are taught early to have desires, to express those desires, to expect the fulfillment of those desires. From a kindergartener's letter to Santa Claus to the high school senior's college admissions application to the mission statement of the entrepreneur applying for a loan, we learn that it is important to say what we want and to assume that we will get it.

But Mick and the boys are right: We can't always get what we want. The video game, the scholarship, the promotion, the house. Sometimes other people get those things instead, leaving us standing in the front yard like mummies trying to understand.

It is good to dream, to desire. It is good to long for and yearn. It is good to reach for that which exceeds one's grasp and then figure out what movement is required to get close enough to clasp it.

What is not good, what will serve only to create frustration and heartache, is wasting a single moment staring into the darkness and trying to figure out why the fog rolled in.

The fog hid the meteor shower; it didn't destroy it. I didn't get to see it, but I still know it's there. And tonight, that has to be enough.

DECEMBER 6, 2009

I was done with court and heading back to the office on a two-lane county road that curves through fields and planted-pine forests, through places that used to be towns and at least one that still is, if only barely. I drove slowly enough to read the signs on the small white churches and nearly slowly enough to count the monster hay bales dotting one side of the road. I felt my shoulders relax and my breath slow.

I passed a pasture, the color of highly-creamed coffee, where a horse stood like a statue staring into the sun. I passed one cotton field foaming with white puffs on skinny brown stalks and then another one, picked over, the stalks looking skinnier in their nakedness. I felt the corners of my mouth ease up into a smile.

Bucolic. Pastoral. Freeze frames of countryside. I'd seen it all before.

But today was different. There was something about the light. Bright, nearly blinding, laser beams from, they tell us, ninety-three million light-years away, it fell at an angle so sharp that the elements in the landscape—wire fences, naked trees, horses—looked like objects in a View-Master, starkly three-dimensional. The blue in the sky was so faded I'd have sworn I could see straight through to the face of God.

I was enthralled.

Could this be December? The month whose only redeeming quality was the placement within its days of Christmas? The month that announces cold, wet weather and chills me to the bone with the mere thought of wearing socks to bed, a pointless but nevertheless irresistible effort at staying warm?

By mid-afternoon it was gone. The luminous, illuminating light was hidden by clouds dense and gray. The view outside my office window was flat like the street facade in the old television westerns and the edges of everything I could see, people and sidewalks and brick corners of buildings, were smudged as though drawn by pencil and unsuccessfully erased.

The rain started within a couple of hours, the clouds wrung out like dirty dishrags, and by the next morning the dirt roads were deep trenches of slick clay. The sky was one endless flannel blanket.

I was, I admit, more than just a bit irritated. I'd been fooled. Made a fool.

That awe-inspiring morning, when the sun spotlighted every tree as though it were the only tree, had been nothing but a tease. That hadn't been the real December. This—the rain and muck and cold—was the real December.

It's important to know what is real. To be able to distinguish diamond from cubic zirconium, sincerity from flattery, truth from lies. I know that. And like anyone who came of age in the Watergate era I've developed a pretty healthy skepticism when it comes to politicians in particular and authority figures in general.

What I've never been able to shake, however, is that hopefulness (some people would call it naiveté) that always anticipates a ninth-inning rally when the lead-off batter draws a walk, that always expects the lost wallet to be returned with the money and the credit cards still inside, that always assumes people will do what they say. So, of course, I saw the first day of December bright and balmy and got seduced into believing I deserved thirty-one days just like that one.

When, I asked myself, gripping the steering wheel and feeling the tires slip violently back and forth through the mud, will I ever learn?

Funny thing: A few hours later, about twelve actually, I stood on the front porch and watched the clouds suddenly take off running, chased by something I couldn't see, and as they ran they left in their wake an unobstructed view of a full moon. Another light. A different kind, but just as enthralling.

When will I ever learn?

DECEMBER 20, 2009

Aden's mama has become a celebrity. She went to New York City last week to promote her business on the "Elevator Pitch" segment of an MSNBC business show. Folks all over the place had the DVRs set for 7:30 in the morning on Sunday and a few of us early risers actually saw the piece through bleary eyes as it aired.

She did well. And, if I had $500,000 to invest, Urban Pirates would get it.

But this isn't about Urban Pirates or venture capital or even the fact that Aden's mama got to meet Howard Dean and sneaked a peak into the Saturday Night Live studio to see her teenage heartthrob Jon Bon Jovi. It is, like all good stories, about clear vision and absolute truth.

A week or so before the trip to the big city, Aden and his mama were out walking in the snow. It was just the two of them and his mama confided to Aden that she was a little nervous about the whole thing.

"Why?" he asked, those huge brown eyes opened wide like a camera aperture letting in all possible light.

"Because," she told him, "I don't want to mess up."

And because she is his mama and she knows that, at seven, his heart is still pure and his thoughts are still true, she asked, "What will I do if I mess up?"

Without a moment's hesitation, he said, "You just come home."

Of course.

We mess up all the time. We make wrong choices. We say things we don't mean. We get lazy and don't live up to our potential. We assume, we presume, we pretend.

And when it's all over, there's only one thing to do: We go home.

I don't remember when I first memorized the famous line from Robert Frost's "The Death of the Hired Man," but I do know that it resonated in me like my own heartbeat. "Home is the place where, when you have to go there, they have to take you in."

Home is the place where, after you've messed up, they still let you in the door without a word of explanation. Home is the place where, after you've made the wrong choice and taken years to figure it out and haven't a clue as to how to make it up to the ones you hurt or even how to say you're sorry, they meet you on the porch with tears of relief in their eyes. Home is the place where, after you've said words that were never true, words that were born of hurt and anger and frustration and can never ever ever be taken back, they come out into the yard, onto the road to pull you in for a feast of fatted calf.

We are all prodigals. Our riotous living may be nothing more than failing to pay attention, but at some point every one of us has left home without a backward glance, secure in—but oblivious to—the reality of home. And every one of us has found him or herself standing on a street corner in some far country—empty, wrung out, used up—when, suddenly, in a moment of clear vision and absolute truth the solution appears like a billboard in Times Square: Home.

It's nearly Christmas, the season in which Christians celebrate the arrival into a less-than-perfect world of one who was himself, in a way, a prodigal. He left his home, emptied himself, used himself up for the good of the other prodigals and, after experiencing the suffering of separation, returned home.

It's the same story. Over and over again. And Aden already understands it. Not bad for a seven-year-old.

"Home is the place where, when you have to go there, they have to take you in." Amen and amen.

POSTSCRIPT

I had absolutely no idea, as I was writing the hundred or so individual pieces that became this book, that they were, in fact, a single narrative. I did not know that I was keeping a travelogue, maintaining a record of one pilgrim's progress. Only in retrospect did it become apparent that the words were weaving, knitting, knotting them into a single seamless garment.

Not long ago a friend invited me into a discussion of a dilemma she was facing. None of the possible resolutions seemed tenable, every path seemed blocked by fallen trees and boulders of one size or the other. She needed to decide, at that particular moment, whether some information she'd received was significant, whether it was a sign pointing her in one direction over another.

I was in the final stages of editing this manuscript and I shared with my friend, not realizing that I was articulating a thesis of sorts, that I had come to the realization that every time I drove somewhere I passed hundreds of signs—street signs, traffic signs, billboards, marquees—but that I actually noticed only those that were pertinent to my particular journey, that somehow my subconscious filtered through all the irrelevant and unimportant to make sure that I saw solely what I needed to see. "So," I told her, "I've come to the conclusion that if I notice it, it's a sign."

So it was that each of the small events and quotidian moments that moved me to search for words was a sign. Each of the hummingbirds, seashells, and full moons was a messenger. Each of the unexpected encounters, delayed arrivals, abrupt departures was there to show me the way.

A long, long time ago a friend and I used to buoy each other through hard times by reciting the things we knew for sure, the things we knew we could depend on no matter what. ("I may not find a job, but Mama and Daddy won't let me go hungry" was always comforting.) The list has grown and shrunk and grown again and, for a while there, it felt as though it was being whittled away to nothing by the same knife that had stabbed me in the heart.

But at that moment, like the cavalry appearing in full gallop just as the circled wagons are about to go up in flame, the words arrived. And the words—most of them factual, all of them true—carried me to safety.

There really are very few things I know for sure anymore, but I have looked long enough and intently enough to know this: When it comes to the completely unstandardized test that is life, there is no prize for being the first one to finish, there is no shame in looking back over my answers, there is a reason why pencils have erasers. And the best part is that there is no proctor hovering in the aisle making sure I don't look to anyone else for answers; I have to decide, no, I get to decide all on my own whether to trust myself or someone else.

Observation is the first step. And with the observation, one can begin to articulate the truth, however difficult it may be. From there, it is simply a matter of breathing and walking around.